S0-AUL-292

STATEMENT CONCERNING PUBLICATIONS OF
RUSSELL SAGE FOUNDATION

The Russell Sage Foundation was established in 1907 by Mrs. Russell Sage "for the improvement of social and living conditions in the United States of America." In carrying out its purpose the Foundation maintains a staff which, among other duties, conducts studies of social conditions, authorized by the General Director, where new information, its analysis and interpretation seem necessary in order to formulate and advance practicable measures aimed at improvement. From time to time the Foundation publishes the results of these studies in book or pamphlet form.

In formulating the problem for study, in mapping out a plan of work on it, in collecting facts, in drawing conclusions, and in the presentation of findings, authors of Foundation studies, who are always either members of the staff or specially commissioned research workers, have the benefit of the criticism and advice of their colleagues in the organization. Full freedom is given research workers for the final decision on all of these steps, and in presenting and interpreting both factual material and conclusions in their own way. While the general responsibility for management of the Foundation is vested in the board of trustees, the responsibility for facts, conclusions, and interpretations rests with the research workers alone and not upon the Foundation, its trustees, or other members of the staff. Publication under the imprint of the Foundation does not imply agreement by the organization or its members with opinions or interpretations of authors. It does imply that care has been taken that the research on which a book is based has been thoroughly done.

30823

SOCIAL WORK
AS A PROFESSION

BY

ESTHER LUCILE BROWN

RESEARCH ASSOCIATE
DEPARTMENT OF STATISTICS
RUSSELL SAGE FOUNDATION

FOURTH EDITION

NEW YORK
RUSSELL SAGE FOUNDATION
1942

DISCARD

Copyright, 1935, 1936, 1938, 1942, by
RUSSELL SAGE FOUNDATION
Printed in the United States of America

———————

First Edition, May, 1935
Second Edition, May, 1936
Third Edition, January, 1938
Fourth Printing, December, 1941
Fourth and Enlarged Edition, November, 1942

E. L. HILDRETH AND COMPANY
printers at Brattleboro, Vermont

TABLE OF CONTENTS

LIST OF TABLES

2

PREFACE

THIS monograph is one of a series dealing with the present status of certain established or emerging professions in the United States. The studies were originally planned for publication as chapters of a single volume comparing conditions in the professions. This plan was abandoned, however, since it seemed probable that they would serve a wider purpose if issued separately. Social Work as a Profession, the first of the series to be published, appeared in 1935, and revised editions were issued in 1936 and 1938. The Professional Engineer and the first edition of Nursing as a Profession were published in 1936. Physicians and Medical Care appeared in 1937, Lawyers and the Promotion of Justice in 1938, and a revised edition of Nursing as a Profession in 1940.

Although there is a large body of literature on the professions, it is often so scattered and sometimes so difficult to obtain that much of it is not used by professional people themselves and even less of it is known to the laity. In these monographs, therefore, significant data obtained from interviews, questionnaires, books, periodicals, and unpublished studies have been assembled and interpreted in such fashion, it is hoped, that the information may be readily utilized by those who are striving to make the professions contribute more widely to the welfare both of their members and of society and also by vocational counselors.

Because it is possible within the compass of a small

volume to present only a fraction of the material relating to the given subject, those facts have been chosen that seem to explain the reasons why a particular group has reached its present degree of effectiveness. No one would dispute the assumption, for example, that today adequate preparation constitutes one of the most important elements of successful practice. So vital is formal training that a large proportion of each monograph has been devoted to a discussion of its evolution and the problems incident to it. Similarly, since professional associations are capable of doing much to raise standards of practice and of determining what the relation of a group to the society it serves shall be, the most important of the national associations are described at some length.

It is generally recognized that one of the most serious problems of the professions is the lack of an accurate determination of the number of persons who are needed in a specific group, and the lack of a form of control that would regulate the numbers to be admitted in the interests of the public and of the group. A corollary to this problem is the uneven distribution of professional service in the various sections of the United States, and the widespread lack of agencies for counseling new members of these professions about selecting localities in which to settle.

There is also the equally important problem of the inability of large numbers of persons receiving low incomes, especially in rural areas, to purchase as much professional service as they need. Even when service is paid for by the government or private philanthropy rather than by the individual, its quantity and quality vary in a marked fashion from one locality to another. In the face of these difficulties, it seemed necessary to set down in each monograph such data as could be obtained on the number of persons engaged in a particular profession, their distribution and earnings, and the demand for their service as compared with the need for it.

In this fourth edition of Social Work as a Profession the original form of presentation has been preserved, but almost all text, except for the first few pages, has been rewritten. Change in social work during the 1930's was profound. We have now been able more nearly to complete the record of that change than was possible in 1938. Census data for the number of social workers in 1940 have recently become available and have been analyzed in some detail; so have additional figures for salaries of social workers. Educational facilities for the training of social workers are springing up throughout the United States. Much ferment is at work within the longer established schools and also within the American Association of Schools of Social Work. This recent growth and revitalization necessitated new evaluation of the purpose and achievement of professional education. Finally, some effort had to be made to interpret the present, and to foresee the possible future, effects of the world cataclysm upon that profession which stands guard over an important sector of social welfare.

SOCIAL WORK AS A PROFESSION

THE HUMANITARIAN MOVEMENT

NO PROFESSION ever makes its appearance full grown and mature. Like all biological organisms, it must undergo augmentation and development. Social work is no exception. If compared with the ministry, teaching, and medicine, it was late in being born. There had been no tradition of professional social work which the Colonists could bring from the Old World and weave into the foundation for a subsequent development here. The New World, moreover, was scarcely ready for it. Human energy had to be expended for many years in the conquest of a hostile environment. Then came the great struggle to push the frontier farther west, to win independence, and to overcome dissension among the states. When America could rest from these efforts, she became absorbed in the growth of industrialism, the expansion of transportation, and the search for new markets. Activity and individualism were everywhere apparent. The teachings and example of a Jesus of Nazareth, a St. Francis of Assisi, and a St. Vincent de Paul pointed the way to service, but the ideal was dimmed by America's zeal to advance her own ends. There was not, however, the picture of poverty and physical suffering that has characterized recent industrial and urban life. Such a picture might have aroused earlier the sympathy of those busy with their own pursuits.

Into a society largely disregardful of the welfare of others, new shoots of social consciousness gradually pushed their way. They flourished and in time grew into the movement of humanitarianism: a movement prophetic of the subsequent profession of social work. The wealthy and middle classes fostered it, and in its name, carried on a variety of activities in behalf of the unfortunate members of the "lower classes." Many of the volunteer workers who thus employed themselves were like the "Mrs. Lee" of Henry Adams' creation. She "plunged into philanthropy, inspected hospitals, read the literature of pauperism and crime, [and] saturated herself with the statistics of vice"[1] for a short time, and then became weary and disillusioned. There were others, however, who developed an abiding interest in charity, and moved steadily forward toward the building of a philosophy of social welfare. To them is due the credit for taking the first steps in the quest for the improvement of the condition of the poor and the socially handicapped.

It was one of the tenets of humanitarianism that there was "an instinct of sympathy" which "prompted to kindly acts." In response to that "instinct," benevolent individuals made generous contributions to philanthropic organizations, and "charity agents" devoted their lives, either without remuneration or for an insignificant sum, to alleviating the distress of the destitute. College men and women studied the "economic aspects of altruism," while cultivating a "humanitarian interest" in convicts, insane, feebleminded, drunkards and "analogously degenerate classes."[2] Rudimentary and even unsound as this humanitarian movement appears to present-day social workers, there emerged from

[1] Adams, Henry, Democracy. Henry Holt and Co., New York, 1933, pp. 2–3.
[2] Warner, Queen, and Harper, American Charities and Social Work. Thomas Y. Crowell Co., New York, 1930, pp. 25–33.

it a group of distinguished pioneers, who not only allied themselves with the immediate problems of the underprivileged, but who sought to discover the causes of distress and a remedy for those causes. Neither their moralistic terminology nor many of their concepts long ago outgrown can obscure the fact that they were a body of able and courageous individuals who assumed the leadership and laid the foundations of a new profession.

Although the humanitarian movement strove to improve the welfare of certain social groups through legislative reforms and the education of public opinion, its major program was concerned with providing material aid for those in need. A few private charitable agencies had appeared in the seventeenth and eighteenth centuries, but it was not until the first half of the nineteenth that relief societies were established in any considerable numbers. They grew up in the more populous cities partly as attempts to eliminate indiscriminate almsgiving by individuals. Some of them gave aid only to particular nationalities; others assisted widows or specific classes of dependents, irrespective of nationality. By 1840 there were over 30 relief-giving societies in the city of New York alone. These associations were instituted "on the principle of providing for particular classes of the indigent, which united moral objects with the relief of physical want."

When, in the winter of 1842–1843, an informally constituted committee made an examination of the work of the New York societies, its report portrayed a situation which undoubtedly existed in other cities and which constituted a serious menace to any sound relief program. The committee noted first of all that the want of discrimination in the giving of relief was a fundamental and very prevalent defect in most charity schemes. Then, too, the societies acted independently of one another. This was a fruitful source of error, inasmuch as the unscrupulous succeeded in obtaining aid from several societies at the same time. Finally, there was no adequate provision for personal intercourse with the recipients at their dwellings nor for the giving of sympathy and counsel.

In order to remedy these difficulties, the New York Association for Improving the Condition of the Poor was organized in 1843. It was followed shortly by similar associations in other cities. Their functions, as conceived, were not to be confined to relief, although they frequently absorbed older and smaller relief societies. Their founders expected that they would promote benevolent enterprises of various kinds. Emphasis was placed upon the "elevation of the physical and moral condition of the indigent," and relief was to be given only when it contributed to moral well-being.

Unfortunately, this goal was largely lost to view as the years progressed. By the end of the seventies, these associations had become for the most part simply relief societies, and often the administration of relief had fallen into such a routine that it was far from realizing its purpose or ideal. Private relief, moreover, whether administered by these associations or by a multiplicity of voluntary agencies, failed to educate the public in intelligent and discriminating methods of giving aid. Public home relief also was wasteful and inefficient. In many places it was lavish, and its administration careless and extravagant, if not corrupt. Some medium for remedying these abuses was necessary,

and the result was the creation of charity organization societies patterned after the distinguished Charity Organisa-
tion Society of London, which had been founded in 1869.

Buffalo established the first complete society in 1877,
seven other societies appeared before the end of 1879, and
by 1892 there were 92. The movement has continued to
the present, although "Family Welfare Society" or some
similar name has generally replaced the earlier phraseology.
The essential features of the program of these groups were
not novel. Certain principles of social welfare were, however, worked out for the first time consistently and the societies have clung to most of them ever since with steadily
increasing faith in their potency. These principles included
investigation, the registration of applicants, co-operation,
adequate relief, and volunteer personal service.[1] These
societies strove to organize "the charitable impulses and
resources of the community on behalf of each family according to its needs, with an endeavor to develop the special
capacities of each individual."[2]

CHANGING CONCEPTS OF SOCIAL WORK

With the experience of the years and the more complete
organization and efficient administration of the private
agencies, there has gradually come a change in the basic
philosophy of charity. Early philanthropists thought largely
in terms of a pauper class, a submerged tenth. Even in con-

[1] Devine, Edward T., Principles of Relief, Macmillan Co., New York,
1914, pp. 314–322, 342–348; Kellogg, Charles D., History of Charity
Organization in the U. S., Press of George H. Ellis, Boston, 1894, pp.
5–12.
[2] Swift, Linton B., "Family Welfare Societies," in Social Work Year
Book, Russell Sage Foundation, New York, 1933, pp. 167–168.

nection with that class, they discriminated between those whom they considered worthy of aid and those who were unworthy. Slowly they abandoned this moralistic concept, and began to think in terms of people on all economic levels whose social relations present difficulties to themselves or to those with whom they are associated. The present era has become increasingly aware of the fact that there are numerous and diverse groups who are not self-sustaining economically, mentally, or morally.[1]

These groups are particularly subject to the vicissitudes of life, and many of them will continue to be so even after society has done everything within its power to minimize chance and hazard. There are the feebleminded and the mentally ill, a large percentage of whom can never be self-supporting nor self-managing. There are the vast numbers of anti-social individuals ranging all the way from those with mild personality difficulties to those who commit the most serious crimes. There are the aged who find themselves without savings; there are orphans, widows with small children, the congenitally handicapped, and wage-earners who are ill or disabled. Besides these individual victims of misfortune, there are those whom capricious natural forces or an unstable economic and social scheme may throw into dependency whenever a catastrophe occurs. A drought or a flood, a war, an economic depression, or even progress in invention and organization may suddenly reduce great numbers of the population to a state of need.[2]

[1] For a brief but authoritative exposition of the evolution of social work, see Lee, Porter R., "Social Work: Cause and Function," in Proceedings of the National Conference of Social Work, 1929, pp. 3–20.

[2] Norton, William J., "What Is Social Work?" in Proceedings of the National Conference of Social Work, 1925, pp. 7–8.

Besides the social worker's recognition of the universality and diversity of human needs and the necessity for conceiving a program broad enough to encompass those needs, advances in the natural and social sciences and changes in philosophical and political concepts have indirectly had important results for social work. The almost total eradication of some diseases and the substantial control of others; the wide extension of the use of natural resources and scientific discoveries; the greater understanding of the individual and society which psychology, psychiatry, anthropology, sociology, and economics have provided—these, and scores of other factors, have had a marked influence upon the scope and method of this new profession.

Changes in the social philosophy of the United States are paving the way for its further alteration. The old belief that the evolution of human society is a mechanical process determined by fate or natural laws incapable of control has almost passed away. The idea is becoming prevalent that this evolution can be studied and, to some extent, guided.[1] Scores of organizations—whether they be the National Resources Planning Board, the Board of Economic Warfare, the federal Department of Agriculture, the Tennessee Valley Authority, councils for the study of post-war reconstruction, state legislative reference bureaus, or councils of social work agencies—are concerning themselves with the plotting of trends and with planning for the future.

The concept of the duty of society to all its members has probably been stronger in recent years than ever before in American life. For a decade the welfare of those suffering

[1] Tufts, James H., Education and Training for Social Work. Russell Sage Foundation, New York, 1923, pp. 13–18.

economic and social disadvantage has been the abiding concern both of the President of the United States and Mrs.
Roosevelt. For an even longer period the Congress has had
a Robert F. Wagner and a LaFollette, who, with tenacity
and courage, have sponsored legislation designed to aid such
persons and groups. As a result of the efforts of both the
executive and the legislative branches of government, a
wide variety of agencies has been created, while others have
been enlarged and revitalized, for the purpose of attempting
to alleviate conditions which produce human distress. The
precept and example of the national government, the extension of federal funds to states with some supervision over
use, the increasing social and political consciousness of the
American people, the growth of the labor movement, and
the assumption of wider responsibilities by social workers
have made their influence felt in the smallest and most remote hamlet.

Where these changes will ultimately lead the United
States is unknown. Recent trends, much accentuated by
the present national emergency, have been consistently in
the direction of a greater degree of governmental planning
and control; not only of the processes of production, distribution, and consumption, but of housing, health services,
education, use of leisure, and public and work assistance.
Many thoughtful persons believe that the present course
will continue, of necessity, after World War II has burned
itself out. There may, however, be a reaction to the philosophy of the present era. This possibility is a matter of grave
concern to such persons, for they fear that a recrudescence
of the individualism of the nineteenth century might run
riot and carry within itself the seeds of social chaos. Even

more they fear the threat of a corporate state in which concern for the welfare of the individual person would cease to exist.

Whatever lies ahead, it is certain that the new profession has been given, of late, the greatest opportunity that has ever come to it to aid in the directing of economic and social change for the benefit of society. And the future welfare of the country will probably be determined, in appreciable measure, by the extent to which social workers can make the governmental and voluntary agencies in which they operate effective instruments for increasing the economic security, as well as the faith and hope of the great mass of the public.

SCOPE OF SOCIAL WORK

The function and scope of contemporary social work must now be examined in more detail. Social work attempts first of all, as it always has done, to provide material assistance for persons who are dependent or in sharp economic distress. It attempts secondly to help such persons individually in their adjustment to their economic and social environment. It is concerned with the psychological problems of clients, whether these problems be the cause or effect of poverty, illness, and crime, or appear independently. Social work seeks furthermore to provide the economically less favored with those amenities of life, such as recreational and cultural activities, which constitute an essential part of an enriched standard of living. It is also interested in raising standards for the entire community, and in recent years has emphasized the desirability of better housing, and enlarged and improved health, education, and leisure-time facilities. Concern for the welfare both of the individual and of the group leads naturally to vigorous participation, if not actually to leadership, in efforts to achieve social reform, whether that reform be more enlightened treatment of the criminal, improvement of wages and conditions of work, protective labor legislation for women and children, extension of economic and political rights to Negroes and other minority groups, or a federally supported and supervised system of public assistance.[1]

These activities fall chiefly within six general categories: case work, group work, administration, research, community organization, and social action. Social case work is the most highly developed, if judged by the relative number of its workers; its professional consciousness as evidenced by membership in the American Association of Social Workers; the emphasis which is placed upon it in professional schools; and the amount of social work literature which has been written about it or by its constituency. Social case work forms the basic program of such agencies as family welfare societies, departments of public assistance, social service departments of hospitals and clinics, visiting teacher departments of schools, probation and parole bureaus, child-placing and protective societies and public agencies, home-service sections of the American Red Cross, travelers' aid societies, and many other agencies.

Social group work is carried on through settlements, community centers, young men's and young women's associations, boys' and girls' clubs, public recreation departments, and other organized recreational and cultural activities.

[1] For a more detailed and particularly helpful discussion of what social work is now seeking to achieve, see Klein, Philip, A Social Study of Pittsburgh, Columbia University Press, New York, 1938, pp. 4–8.

Administration and research are techniques, not peculiar to social work, that nevertheless are being increasingly studied and adapted to use within the wide range of social work agencies. Community organization includes social planning and the promotion of programs fostered by councils of social agencies, community chests, state and national supervisory and advisory agencies, public welfare departments, and public health and health educational agencies.

Social action, the area of least uniformity of definition and purpose, is essentially the area of social reform. It includes promotion of social experimentation preceding legal action, as well as legislation designed to establish new modes of living and acting together. Like administration and research, it also is not peculiarly an area of social work. It is undertaken by some social work organizations exercising chiefly other functions, such as the American Association of Social Workers and state conferences of social work, and by such periodicals as The Survey and Social Work Today. It is promoted more extensively by groups organized for the express purpose of accomplishing reform, such as child labor committees, consumers' leagues, housing associations, co-operative societies, and associations for legislation.

Perhaps nothing is more suggestive of the scope of social work than a list of the associate and special groups that were scheduled to meet in 1941 at the National Conference of Social Work held in Atlantic City.[1] Although the list varies somewhat from year to year, it is an index of the type of independent associations which are increasingly allying themselves with the enhancement of social welfare. The

[1] "National Conference of Social Work and Associate Groups," in the Conference Bulletin, April, 1941, pp. 19–40.

following organizations include many whose activities are at the very heart of social work, as well as some which are on the periphery.

1. American Association for Applied Psychology
2. American Association of Medical Social Workers
3. American Association on Mental Deficiency
4. American Association of Personal Finance Companies, Committee on Social Relations
5. American Association of Psychiatric Social Workers
6. American Association of Schools of Social Work
7. American Association of Social Workers
8. American Association for the Study of Group Work
9. American Association of Visiting Teachers
10. American Council on Community Self-Help Exchanges
11. American Foundation for the Blind
12. American Home Economics Association, Social Welfare and Public Health Department
13. American Legion, National Child Welfare Division
14. American Public Welfare Association
15. American Red Cross
16. Association of the Junior Leagues of America
17. Birth Control Federation of America
18. Child Welfare League of America
19. Church Conference of Social Work
20. Committee on Supervised Homemaker Service
21. Committee on Unmarried Parenthood
22. Conference on Immigration Policy
23. Episcopal Social Work Conference
24. Family Welfare Association of America
25. Home Missions Council of North America
26. Indian Affairs Forum
27. Joint Committee of Trade Unions in Social Work
28. Legal Aid Group
29. Life Insurance Adjustment Bureau
30. National Association for Aid to Dependent Children

31. National Association of Day Nurseries
32. National Association of Goodwill Industries
33. National Association of Training Schools
34. National Board, Y.W.C.A.'s
35. National Child Labor Committee
36. National Committee on Big Brother and Big Sister Service
37. National Committee for Mental Hygiene
38. National Committee on Volunteers in Social Work
39. National Conference of Jewish Social Welfare
40. National Council on Naturalization and Citizenship
41. National Council, Y.M.C.A.'s
42. National Federation of Settlements
43. National Girls' Work Council
44. National Institute Conference of International Institutes, Local Councils and Leagues for the Foreign-Born
45. National Probation Association
46. National Social Work Club Committee
47. National Society for Crippled Children
48. National Society for the Prevention of Blindness
49. National Travelers Aid Association
50. National Tuberculosis Association
51. Salvation Army
52. Social Case Work Council
53. Social Service Exchange Committee
54. Social Work Publicity Council
55. Social Work Today
56. Social Work Vocational Bureau
57. State Conference Secretaries
58. Survey Associates

IS SOCIAL WORK A PROFESSION?

The word "profession" was once generally understood to be a generic term for the ministry, law, and medicine. Other vocations such as teaching, engineering, architecture, and dentistry have come to be widely accepted as professions even by those who define the term narrowly. Besides these, there are scores of groups who designate their occupations as professional. Musicians, actors, journalists, librarians, and registered nurses make only the beginning of a list which is constantly growing longer. It is a matter of interest to the student of society to note the zeal with which members of multifarious occupations wish to be known as professional, even though they have no understanding of the meaning and significance of the term. The reason lies in the fact that such a high degree of prestige has long been attached to the older professions that many vocations are desirous of attaining it.

The demands of a twentieth century society are indirectly helping these groups to achieve their goal. Much emphasis is being placed upon the greater utilization of scientific knowledge, longer educational and occupational training, and a higher motive of service for the good of all. Insistence in such directions is certain to result in forcing many vocations to move toward professionalism.

At the present moment, as a consequence both of their own desire and of social pressure, several occupations are well on the way to attaining full professional status. Social work is undoubtedly one of these. Such status can be won, however, only on the basis of its ability to meet several rigid tests. According to Dr. Abraham Flexner's frequently quoted criteria of true professions: (1) they involve essentially intellectual operations accompanied by large individual responsibility; (2) they are learned in nature, and their members are constantly resorting to the laboratory and seminar for a fresh supply of facts; (3) they are not merely academic and theoretical, however, but are definitely practical in their aims; (4) they possess a technique capable of communication through a highly specialized educational discipline; (5) they are self-organized, with activities, duties, and responsibilities which completely engage their participants and develop group consciousness; and finally (6) they are likely to be more responsive to public interest than are unorganized and isolated individuals and they tend to become increasingly concerned with the achievement of social ends.[1]

When the long list of occupations which are applicants for professional status is examined in the light of these six requirements, it is evident that the percentage of elimination must be high. The sixth criterion alone is fatal to many groups whose members are well trained and well organized but whose primary motive is one of self-interest. On this score, social work has nothing to fear. Aside from the ministry, probably no group has ever been more concerned with the general welfare. Social work has also conformed for a long period to three other criteria. It has a self-consciousness, fostered particularly by social caseworkers, which is readily apparent in the large attendance at the National Conference of Social Work and at state conferences; in the growing membership of the American Association of Social Workers and its local chapters; and in the recent appearance of organizations designed for the professional and economic advancement of all employes of social agencies. It is intensely practical in its aims—so practical in fact that

[1] "Is Social Work a Profession?" in Proceedings of the National Conference of Charities and Correction, 1915, pp. 578–581.

For a further definition of "professions," see Whitehead, Alfred N., Adventures of Ideas, Macmillan Co., New York, 1933, pp. 71–79; Carr-Saunders, A. M., and Wilson, P. A., The Professions, Clarendon Press, Oxford, 1933, p. 491.

it has often been criticized for partially neglecting the search for general principles and the creation of a broad social philosophy which might form a solid foundation for practice. Its subject material comes, at least in part, from science and learning: from economics, sociology, biology, psychology, psychiatry, religion, medicine, law—all of these might possibly be utilized more extensively than they are—and from a literature which it is gradually building for itself.

Concerning the ability of social work to qualify as a profession on the basis of the individual responsibility which its constituency assumes, Dr. Flexner was in doubt in 1915 when he addressed social workers at the National Conference. He visualized social work as a mediating agency, which investigated and analyzed a problem, and then referred it to the specialized agency best equipped to handle it. The difference, however, between this commitment of responsibility by the social worker and by the general practitioner in any field, who must turn to the expert, is perhaps one of degree rather than kind. Initial responsibility rests extensively with the social worker, and also final responsibility to the extent, at least, of seeing that the problem is carried through to some conclusion. The increasing advent of trained workers, the growth of case- and group-work techniques, and the exigencies of the past few years have greatly augmented the responsibility which social work has assumed. As one views this vocation in the year 1942, it seems fairly evident that it has progressed far in the direction of professional status, when measured by this criterion.

This does not mean, however, that every social worker is professional, or even near-professional, either on the score of the degree of responsibility taken or on other counts. This is so evident that the American Association of Social Workers has limited its membership to those who are able to meet the requirements which it has decided upon as defining a "professional social worker."[1] These requirements automatically exclude a large percentage of all social workers. It is chiefly through the efforts of a body of executives, supervisors, and trained staff workers, who form the professional nucleus, that the status of social work has been raised.

The extent to which this occupation has, within the last two decades, developed a literature and a method capable of being transmitted by an educational system is distinctly encouraging. Induction into social work was so long by apprenticeship—it still is to a considerable degree—that insistence upon training in schools of social work has been hindered and delayed. Even now, with an active American Association of Schools of Social Work and 42 institutions recognized by it, besides many nascent schools which are not yet members of the national organization, the problem of what should constitute the subject matter for the technical training course still looms large. Enough has been achieved, however, in the selection and co-ordination of subject material and the creation of a literature to justify the feeling among social workers that they have at least come close to meeting this final requirement for professional rank.

EVOLUTION OF TRAINING FOR SOCIAL WORK

Probably no other factor is so important to the future of social work, from both the angle of the complete achieve-

[1] See pp. 116–118.

ment of professionalism and that of efficiency of service to society, as adequate academic and vocational preparation.

Before the beginning of the twentieth century, opportunities for professional training were exceedingly slight: schools of social work had not yet appeared and apprenticeship was the best the social agencies had to offer. Although there was a growing recognition of the need for training, men and women were all too often appointed to positions, not on the merit of the contribution they would be able to render society, but because they themselves were in need of financial aid. In a paper which Mary E. Richmond read before the Civic Club in Philadelphia in 1897, she said:

It seems sheer waste of time to say anything at this late day about the need of training in charitable work, and yet I have learned that philanthropy is still one of those disorganized branches of human knowledge in which he who takes anything for granted is lost. . . . "You ask me," wrote a clergyman, "what qualifications Miss —— has for the position of agent in the charity organization society. She is a most estimable lady, and the sole support of her widowed mother. It would be a real charity to give her the place." Another applicant for the same position when asked whether she had had any experience in charity work replied that she had had a good deal. She had sold tickets for church fairs. Though these particular ladies were not employed, is it not still a very common thing to find charity agents who have been engaged for no better reason, like one who was employed to distribute relief, because he had failed in the grocery business? And with our volunteer service it is no better. In no other field are good intentions permitted to play such havoc.[1]

[1] The Long View. Papers and Addresses by Mary E. Richmond. Selected and edited by Joanna C. Colcord and Ruth Z. S. Mann. Russell Sage Foundation, New York, 1930, p. 86.

Perhaps the first public recognition that professional training was necessary had come through a paper read by Anna L. Dawes in Chicago in 1893 before the International Congress of Charities, Correction and Philanthropy. She asserted that, with the extension of charity organization societies beyond the large cities to the small cities and towns, it was almost impossible to find "suitable" men or women as secretaries for the work. Since practically the whole success of the undertaking depended upon the officers who administered its affairs, this lack of efficient executives created a very serious problem. Miss Dawes was convinced that this situation arose, not from a lack of willing men and women, but from a lack of opportunity for training. She advocated:

. . . some course of study where an intelligent young person can add to an ordinary education such branches as may be necessary for this purpose, with a general view of those special studies in political and social science which are most closely connected with the problem of poverty; and where both he and his associate, already learned in the study of books, can be taught what is now the alphabet of charitable science—some knowledge of its underlying ideas, its tried and trusted methods, and some acquaintance with the various devices employed for the upbuilding of the needy, so that no philanthropic undertaking from a model tenement-house to a kindergarten or a sand heap will be altogether strange to his mind. Some more immediately practical experience of the work likely to be required should also be given, some laboratory practice in the science of charity, if we may so speak.[1]

It was not until five years after Miss Dawes had pointed out the need for training that the first school of social work

[1] "The Need of Training Schools for a New Profession," in Seventh Session of the International Congress of Charities, Correction and Philanthropy, Chicago, June, 1893, p. 19.

made its appearance, and it was not until nearly a quarter of a century later that schools were sufficient in number to provide any considerable nucleus of trained workers. In the meantime, however, certain methods were devised which gave the inexperienced some insight into the nature of social work. By watching older visitors, by talking to executives, and by attending conferences, new workers learned something of the art of helping those in need. Shortly after these first steps had been taken, a few of the agencies began to arrange lectures and courses in reading. In time these plans developed into an apprenticeship training whereby beginners were initiated more gradually and systematically into the practice of social work. Family welfare societies[1] and some of the children's agencies succeeded in building up the apprenticeship system on a large scale. As schools of social work have advanced, apprenticeship has been gradually diminishing. It still survives, however, in private agencies where salaries are low and where the chances of promotion do not attract the professionally trained, and in certain sections of the country where the number of graduates of social work schools is altogether inadequate. In the public agencies various experiments for the supervision of case work and for "training-on-the-job" have been instituted. These experiments, however, have rarely constituted a system of apprenticeship training. Some of the public agencies are now attempting to recruit as many persons with professional education as possible.

Many people still believe that apprenticeship provides

[1] For an exposition of present concepts of apprenticeship education, see Report of the Committee on Training: Training in Family Social Work Agencies, Family Welfare Association of America, New York, March, 1933.

reasonably competent service for a single field of work. This is probably true if individuals are trained to carry only the more routine tasks of their particular fields. It is debatable, however, whether apprenticeship can give the broader point of view which executives of even highly specialized agencies need. Beyond preparation for a single type of work, the question of its value becomes much greater. Can it provide individuals with the knowledge or the adaptability which will enable them to transfer easily from one division of social work to another? As Miss Abbott has pointed out, it is narrow in scope; it is costly to the agency; and its students frequently suffer from the lack of time which busy administrators can find for educational instruction.[1] Even the administrative ranks of social work, however, are still very largely occupied by people who have had no professional training. Many of them entered the field before schools of social work were accessible, and they were obliged to learn on the job. In spite of the great success which a large number of them have attained, they declare that they regret the fact that they have not had formal preparation. Were they to enter the profession today, they would probably come to it with a degree from a school of social work.

Apprenticeship in the twentieth century, as preparation for professional work, can be scarcely regarded as other than an anachronism. It may not have been ill-suited to the needs of a young and simple type of society. One doubts whether it can be made to function effectively, however, when organization has become complex and when time is a costly

[1] Abbott, Edith, "Education for Social Work," in Social Work Year Book, 1933, pp. 142–143.

27

commodity. Less than a half-century ago great lawyers were trained through reading in a law office under the guidance of their superiors. Today such training is almost extinct and when found, it is considered the poorest possible preparation for entering upon the practice of law. Group after group has relinquished apprenticeship as an outmoded method. Remnants of it still appear, however, both in social work and in nursing. As the former profession has gradually become more conscious of the fact that apprenticeship has long since served its purpose, many social workers have attempted to insist that it be replaced by preparation in accredited schools. This was an impossible task in the early 1930's because of the sudden influx of thousands of emergency workers in public welfare agencies. Their need for training beyond the very elementary instruction which the agencies found time to give them was so apparent, however, that steps were taken by federal and state organizations to provide some proportion of those expected to assume executive and supervisory responsibilities with at least a minimum of formal training in recognized schools of social work. Chaotic and discouraging as conditions appeared, the situation lent actual impetus to the movement for professional education.

SCHOOLS OF SOCIAL WORK

Before the National Conference of Charities and Correction in 1915, Felix Frankfurter uttered a statement which might well be taken as the "articles of faith" of the profession which he addressed. No social worker has offered a more logical argument than he for the need of preparation for social work comparable to the preparation for law and medicine:

> I submit that what has been found necessary for adequate training for those social activities which we call the professions of law and medicine is needed for the very definite, if undefined, profession we call social work. I cannot believe that the preliminary training of a lawyer, most of his life spent in the adjustment of controversies between individuals, requires less of a background, less of an understanding of what has gone before in life, less of a rigorous critical discipline than is needed by those of you who go out to pass judgment on the social conditions of whole communities, by those of you who administer laws like the minimum wage law, and the other social legislation now administered in great numbers by social workers. Secondly, I cannot believe that a training fit to discipline people who shall guide and deal with the social forces of the day, can be done in less time than the time found necessary for the training of lawyers. Thirdly, I cannot believe that the experience of medicine and law as to the quality of teachers to train men in those professions applies less in regard to teachers of social work. I believe social workers, to reach the professional level, must be guided by teachers not only of insight and possessed of scientific equipment, but teachers who give their whole time and thought to it.[1]

It was the growing realization of that need to which Mr. Frankfurter referred in 1915, which had resulted seventeen years previously in the rudimentary beginnings of the first school of social work. In the summer of 1898 the New York Charity Organization Society took initial steps in the direction of a professional school by holding a six weeks' training course, designed primarily to increase the efficiency of social workers already in the field. In 1903 the training

---

[1] "Social Work and Professional Training," in Proceedings of the National Conference of Charities and Correction, 1915, p. 595.

program was extended to include a six months' winter session, which provided weekly lectures at a late afternoon hour. The following year these experimental training classes developed into the New York School of Philanthropy, and a full year's course of training was instituted, which was planned primarily for students without experience in social work. In Chicago the movement to establish professional training was led by Graham Taylor of Chicago Commons, who took a prominent part in the development of the Chicago Institute of Social Science. This was opened in 1901, as a part of the Extension Division of the University of Chicago. In the fall of 1904, Boston began a similar undertaking under the title "School for Social Workers, maintained by Simmons College and Harvard University." The success of the schools of social work in New York, Chicago, and Boston stimulated agencies in Philadelphia to provide a training course in that city for the preparation of their own workers. In 1908 a special training class was held, which was organized the following year as the Philadelphia Training School for Social Work. In St. Louis the movement to provide formal instruction appeared almost contemporaneously with its rise in the eastern cities. In 1908 the first full year's course was begun. The school was established by social workers of the city in order to provide training facilities for themselves, but was closely affiliated with the University of Missouri.

Thus before 1910, there were schools in the five largest cities of the country. Seven years later World War I lent impetus to social work instruction. Emergency training courses in home services were given in co-operation with the American Red Cross in 15 universities, most of which had previously undertaken no practical preparation for social work. In order that the courses might be as uniform as possible in quantity and content, the Red Cross outlined the subject matter, prescribed standards, supplemented the teaching personnel of the university, and usually assumed responsibility for the field work of the students. These home-service institutes demonstrated the need for training facilities in sections of the country where schools had not existed and were an important factor in stimulating the interest of universities in education for social work.[1]

Subsequent to the war, the number of schools increased so rapidly that in 1928, when Sydnor H. Walker made her study of Social Work and the Training of Social Workers, she found 35 institutions in the United States and Canada with organized curricula for full-time students which she classified as schools of social work.[2] What the number is at present cannot be easily determined. There are now 42 schools that have been approved for membership in the American Association of Schools of Social Work. They will be referred to in the following discussions as "approved" schools. Only about institutions belonging to that Association is there any extensive information available either to social workers or to other interested persons. Hence discussion, except in the next section, will center around them.

EVOLVING CURRICULA OF SOCIAL WORK

Before examining the schools that hold membership in the Association, attention must be centered briefly upon

[1] For the only substantial account available of the early development of schools of social work, see Steiner, Jesse F., Education for Social Work, University of Chicago Press, Chicago, 1921.
[2] University of North Carolina Press, Chapel Hill, 1928, p. 132.

those other colleges and universities that have made provision for varying amounts of training in social work. After examination of recent bulletins, these additional American institutions of higher learning that were found to offer social work courses were classified in four groups. To Group I were assigned 22 colleges and universities whose programs of training appeared to be most nearly comparable to the curricula approved by the national organization,[1] or to have progressed farther along the road toward becoming "schools" than had the other courses of study. A brief note about the curriculum and the number of students enrolled in each of these 22 schools is presented in the Appendix. The list of institutions selected is as follows:

Adelphi College, Graduate School of Social Work, Garden City, N. Y.

Alabama, University of, Department of Sociology, Tuscaloosa

Arkansas, University of, Department of Social Welfare, Fayetteville

Florida State College for Women, Department of Sociology and Social Work, Tallahassee

Illinois, University of, Curriculum in Social Administration, Urbana

Kentucky, University of, Department of Social Work, Lexington

Michigan State College, Graduate Curriculum in Social Work of Department of Sociology, East Lansing

Mills College, Graduate Curriculum in Social Work, Oakland, Calif.

Missouri, University of, Department of Sociology, Columbia

North Dakota, University of, Professional Course in Social Work of Department of Sociology, Grand Forks

[1] See pp. 104–105 for statement of requirements for membership in the Association.

Notre Dame, University of, Department of Social Work, Notre Dame, Ind.

South Carolina, University of, School of Social Work, Columbia

Temple University, Department of Social Group Work, Philadelphia

Utah State Agricultural College, Graduate Division of Social Work, Logan

Wisconsin, University of, Department of Sociology and Anthropology, Madison

Xavier University, School of Social Service, New Orleans

COLLEGES OFFERING TRAINING FOR Y.M.C.A. AND OTHER GROUP WORK OR FOR CHURCH SOCIAL WORK

George Williams College, Professional Division, Chicago

Scarritt College for Christian Workers, Department of Social Work, Nashville

Schauffler College of Religious and Social Work, Cleveland

Springfield College, Social Science Division, Springfield, Mass.

Whittier College, Y.M.C.A. Graduate Training for Secretaryship, Whittier, Calif.

Willamette University, Department of Sociology and Anthropology, Salem, Ore.

A few of these educational institutions offer training exclusively on the graduate level; others offer both graduate and undergraduate instruction. The course of study is, in the majority of instances, under the supervision of an administrative unit created for that purpose. In a few institutions it remains within the department of sociology that gave it birth. Some two-thirds of these curricula are concerned with the general field of social work, but four were designed expressly to provide training for the Y.M.C.A. and other forms of group work, and two for church social work. Two of the universities included in this group once held membership in the American Association of Schools of Social Work; several of the others have arranged their course of study to conform with the requirements of that organization for a Type I school.[1] Most of these curricula have small enrollments, and their future existence is so precarious that some of them will not be offered in 1942–1943. George Williams College, however, provides professional education which is probably on a more secure financial and administrative basis than is that of many of the schools within the Association, while the Department of Social Work of Scarritt College is about to become part of a new school of social work operated jointly by Vanderbilt University, George Peabody College, and Scarritt College.

In Group II have been listed 14 other colleges and universities that announce, through their bulletins, a sequence of courses in social work. These courses are almost without exception within departments of sociology. Most are on the undergraduate level, but occasionally some graduate instruction is added. Supplementary information about them also appears in the Appendix. They are as follows:

Akron, University of, Akron, Ohio
Alabama College [State College for Women], Montevallo
Georgia State College for Women, Milledgeville
John Carroll University, Cleveland
Marquette University, Milwaukee
Montana, University of, Missoula
Mount Saint Mary's College, Los Angeles
New Hampshire, University of, Durham

[1] See Table 1, p. 41, for definition of the Association's Type I and Type II schools.

Ohio University, Athens
Saint Michael's College, Winooski Park, Vermont
Sam Houston State Teachers College, Huntsville, Texas
San Francisco State College, San Francisco
South Dakota, University of, Vermillion
Texas Christian University, Fort Worth

At least 18 institutions of higher learning, furthermore, offer three or four undergraduate courses in social work. Their names appear in the Appendix under Group III. Finally, we have placed in Group IV, without including their names, no fewer than 94 colleges and universities in which one undergraduate course, generally a survey of the field of social work, was announced. In several instances a second course was noted, and sometimes a third, the content of which might be predominantly either social work or sociology.

The above classification is inexact and unsatisfactory. There are perhaps curricula which were not discovered, while some of those noted may have had no students and some may have passed out of existence before this study is off the press. Many colleges or informed persons would probably disagree with some of the assignments made in this classification. Had visits to these institutions been possible, different decisions would undoubtedly have been made. Information gathered from bulletins and even from correspondence is slight and sometimes misleading. Hence, no great reliance can be placed upon the Appendix data relating to a specific institution or to the classification of that institution.

In spite of these shortcomings, however, we are of the opinion that this rudimentary attempt to list and classify curricula of social work has real value. It reveals the fact that very extensive development of training is in process of evolution. Because discussion in the past has been largely confined to those schools that were members of the national organization, no comprehensive picture has existed of the scope of this development. Now and again a school withdrew from the Association, and a new one was added. The impression gained, however, was of a situation far more static than was true. In reality, the situation is exceedingly dynamic; ferment is at work throughout the country. While the back is turned for a moment, another course in training pushes up its head, exactly as do curricula in training for public administration. And like these, the soil in which it has been planted is frequently so poor and arid that death comes early.

To departments of sociology must be given credit for having created most of the curricula of social work that have developed into autonomous schools or that are in process of such evolution. Painstaking labor and long devotion have gone to this task. Some of the courses of study listed above will, like their predecessors, be cultivated and nourished until they are able to stand alone. But many a department of sociology has introduced such courses without careful consideration of the needs of the immediate region for more training facilities, or of its ability to furnish substantial professional education. This practice becomes increasingly deleterious as standards of social work are raised, and as approved schools of social work grow in number and ability to perform their function.

Except in universities whose budgets permit large and competent faculties of sociology and anthropology, or where other opportunities for the education of social workers are so few that the department has real obligation to provide training, the introduction of social work courses is deleterious for another reason. It robs sociologists of time and money that should be used to strengthen the scientific base on which social work rests. A subsequent section will discuss the need of students of social work for both broad and intensive preprofessional training in the social sciences, and particularly in sociology. Any supplementary effort which deflects the energy of sociologists tends to retard progress in a field of knowledge of incomparable importance for social workers. So great is the confusion about the purpose of the undergraduate college, however, that some educational institutions whose bulletins announce the most meager offerings in sociology and social anthropology have attempted to introduce several courses in social work. One can only conclude that such courses are given in place of fundamental social science courses for which there can be no desirable substitute.

If many colleges are doing themselves and the profession of social work an injustice by permitting social work courses to be offered at all, there are others that can justify their effort because of the urgent need for some training of social workers in regions where sufficient provision for professional education has not previously existed. There is, for example, the territory south of Chapel Hill and Louisville and east of St. Louis and New Orleans, whose only approved school is Atlanta University, in service to colored students. There are also the vast stretches of 13 states west of the Mississippi River, including the "Empire" of Texas, where there is not yet one school holding membership in the Association. For efforts to undertake training in these areas, commendation is often richly deserved. Unfortunately, the efforts have not infrequently been doomed to failure, or have been rewarded only by very small enrollments of students, because of the economic and cultural milieu in which they have been made. Over and over correspondents have written to the author the same distressing tale of the paucity of trained social workers and the smallness of salaries in their region. They note that the great majority of those persons designated as "social workers" have had no professional training even on an undergraduate level, and in some states many have not had a college education.

To build a school of social work in a state that is predominantly rural with a scattered population, or that is backward economically and culturally, is a difficult task. And yet it is in these very places that the greatest need exists for competent workers and for leaders who can raise social work to a level where it will effectively contribute to the solution of long existent problems. Many persons intimately acquainted with conditions in such areas believe that the most immediate solution of the question of recruitment of a trained social work personnel is undergraduate professional education, accompanied by provision for advanced work for the relatively few students who can be encouraged to continue their studies. Such persons know that the best social work practice can be obtained only as the result of a prolonged educational process. Faced with the exigencies of their situation, however, they conceive of undergraduate training as an almost necessary evolutionary step toward graduate training. And they gain some comfort from the knowledge that, notwithstanding the relatively high percentage of students who voluntarily enter with the baccalaureate degree, only five out of 76 approved medical schools and eight out of 101 approved law schools require the degree for admission.

Although universities struggling with the problem of social work training, particularly in the South and the West, are in want of encouragement and assistance, few of their curricula meet the present requirements for approval of the American Association of Schools of Social Work. Hence these universities find themselves deprived of such professional aid and stimulus as the national organization provides its constituency, and forced to get on as best they can without official recognition. So valuable would the Association's influence be that it seems both feasible and desirable that the Association make a place within its structure which needed schools predominantly on the undergraduate level could occupy with honor and dignity. Thereby the accrediting body could help such schools in their transition toward complete graduate status, and could contribute largely to the upbuilding of social work in undeveloped regions.

ASSOCIATION SCHOOLS

Having set down such information as was possible about the development of curricula of social work that are not recognized by the American Association of Schools of Social Work, we now turn to those 42 schools that hold membership in the national body. Examination of Table 1 reveals that all of them, except the Montreal School of Social Work which maintains informal co-operative arrangements with McGill University, are either affiliated with or are integral parts of universities. The movement to bring existing schools of social work under the aegis of a university and to create new schools only under such auspices has progressed rapidly in late years. Impetus is now being lent to the movement by the action of the Association in 1939, which decreed that thereafter any school desiring membership should be part of a college or university approved by the Association of American Universities.

At present 15 of the schools are connected with state colleges or universities, including the University of Toronto and the University of Hawaii which are technically provincial and territorial rather than state institutions. The school in Louisville is part of a municipal university, as is that of Wayne University in Detroit. Twenty-five schools are attached to private colleges and universities. Within the last group are six Catholic schools, and two operated primarily for Negro students.

The reader should not infer that, because these schools are now within the university fold, their ties with the parent organization are necessarily strong. The New York School and the Pennsylvania School, long independent, are affiliated with Columbia University and the University of Pennsylvania, respectively, and their graduates receive the degrees of those institutions. In most essential respects, however, these two schools, which have remained physically apart from their universities, may still be considered independent in administration, in the planning of their curricula, and financially. Both have boards of trustees on which university representation is smaller than that of social work, and the New York School continues to be, administratively and financially, a part of the Community Service

SCHOOLS OF SOCIAL WORK

TABLE I.—LIST OF 42 SCHOOLS HAVING MEMBERSHIP IN
AMERICAN ASSOCIATION OF SCHOOLS OF SOCIAL WORK,
MAY, 1942; DATES OF ESTABLISHMENT AND OF
ADMISSION; AND RECOGNITION CONFERRED[a]

**TYPE I. SCHOOLS OFFERING A MINIMUM OF ONE YEAR OF
GRADUATE PROFESSIONAL TRAINING. (7 SCHOOLS)**

Hawaii, University of, Department of Social Work Training, Honolulu.
1936. 1942. Grants certificate.

Howard University, Graduate Division of Social Work, Washington,
D.C. 1935. 1940. Grants certificate.

Louisiana State University, Graduate School of Public Welfare Administration, Baton Rouge. 1937. 1940. Grants M.A. degree.

Oklahoma, University of, School of Social Work, Norman. 1917.
1938. Grants M.A. degree; also certificate.

Utah, University of, School of Social Work, Salt Lake City. 1938.
1940. Grants M.A. and certificate.

Washington, State College of, Graduate School of Social Work, Pull-
man. 1938. 1942. Grants certificate.

West Virginia University, Department of Social Work, Morgantown.
1939. 1942. Grants certificate.

**TYPE II. SCHOOLS OFFERING A MINIMUM OF TWO YEARS
OF GRADUATE PROFESSIONAL TRAINING. (35 SCHOOLS)**

Atlanta University, School of Social Work, Atlanta. 1920. 1928.
Grants degree of Master of Social Work; also diploma.

Boston College, School of Social Work, Boston. 1936. 1938. Grants
degree of M.S. in Social Work.

Boston University, School of Social Work, Boston. 1936. 1939.
Grants degree of M.S. in Social Service.

Bryn Mawr College, Carola Woerishoffer Graduate Department of Social Economy and Social Research, Bryn Mawr, Pa. 1915. 1919.
C.M. Grants M.A. and Ph.D. degrees; also certificate.

[a] The first of the two dates for each school indicates the "year of establishment";
the second, the year of admission to the Association; C.M. indicates charter member.
The year of establishment is, in many instances, difficult to determine because of the
paucity of records and the several interpretations given the term. We chose the earli-
est date for each school which was recorded in its bulletin. When no date was given,
secondary sources were consulted. In the case of the older schools, the dates generally
refer either to the short courses or to the few isolated courses in social work then
given. These fragments of training generally evolved into well-defined curricula. In
several universities, however, early undertakings were discontinued, and new schools
of social work were created only after a period of years.

41

TABLE I (*Continued*)

Buffalo, University of, School of Social Work, Buffalo. 1931. 1934. Grants degree of Master of Social Service; also certificate.

California, University of, Department of Social Welfare, Berkeley. 1919. 1928. Grants M.A. and Ph.D. degrees; also certificate.

Carnegie Institute of Technology, Department of Social Work, Pittsburgh. 1914. 1919. C.M. Grants degree of Master of Social Work.

Catholic University of America, School of Social Work, Washington, D.C. 1934. 1937. Grants degree of M.S. in Social Work and doctor's degree in Social Science.

Chicago, University of, School of Social Service Administration, Chicago. 1901. 1919. C.M. Grants M.A. and Ph.D. degrees.

Denver, University of, Department of Social Work, Denver. 1931. 1933. Grants M.A. degree.

Fordham University, School of Social Service, New York City. 1916. 1929. Grants M.A. degree; also diploma.

Indiana University, Training Course for Social Work, Bloomington. 1911. 1923. Grants M.A. degree.

Louisville, University of, Graduate Division of Social Administration, Louisville, Kentucky. 1935. 1937. Grants degree of M.S. in Social Administration; also certificate.

Loyola University, School of Social Work, Chicago. 1914. 1921. Grants degree of Master of Social Work.

Michigan, University of, Curriculum in Social Work, Ann Arbor. 1921. 1922. Grants degree of Master of Social Work.

Minnesota, University of, Graduate Course in Social Work, Minneapolis. 1917. 1919. C.M. Grants M.A. in Social Work and Ph.D. degrees; also certificate.

Montreal School of Social Work, Montreal, Canada. Some co-operative arrangement with McGill University. 1919. 1919. Withdrew from Association in 1928; readmitted in 1939. Grants diploma.

National Catholic School of Social Service, Washington, D.C. Affiliated with Catholic University of America. 1921. 1923. Grants degree of M.S. in Social Work; also diploma.

Nebraska, University of, Graduate School of Social Work, Lincoln. 1908. 1940. Grants degree of M.S. in Social Work; also certificate.

New York School of Social Work, New York City. Affiliated with Columbia University. 1898. 1919. C.M. Grants M.A. degree; also diploma.

TABLE I (*Continued*)

North Carolina, University of, Division of Public Welfare and Social Work, Chapel Hill. 1920. 1920. Withdrew from Association in 1932; readmitted in 1936.

Ohio State University, School of Social Administration, Graduate Program, Columbus. 1906. 1919. C.M. Grants degree of M.A. in Social Administration.

Pennsylvania School of Social Work, Philadelphia. Affiliated with University of Pennsylvania. 1908. 1919. C.M. Grants degree of Master of Social Work; also certificate.

Pittsburgh, University of, School of Applied Social Science, Pittsburgh. 1919. 1919. Withdrew from Association in 1922; readmitted in 1934. Grants degree of M.S. in Social Administration.

St. Louis University, School of Social Service, St. Louis. 1930. 1933. Grants degree of M.S. in Social Work.

Simmons College, School of Social Work, Boston. 1904. 1919. C.M. Grants M.S. degree.

Smith College School of Social Work, Northampton, Massachusetts. 1918. 1919. C.M. Grants degree of Master of Social Science.

Southern California, University of, School of Social Work, Los Angeles. 1920. 1922. Grants degree of Master of Social Work; also certificate.

Toronto, University of, Department of Social Science, Toronto, Canada. 1914. 1919. Withdrew from Association in 1928; readmitted in 1939. Grants diploma.

Tulane University, School of Social Work, New Orleans. 1914. 1927. Grants degree of Master of Social Work.

Washington, University of, Graduate School of Social Work, Seattle. 1919. 1934. Grants M.A. degree.

Washington University, George Warren Brown Department of Social Work, St. Louis. 1925. 1928. Grants degree of Master of Social Work; also Bachelor of Science in Public Administration.

Wayne University, School of Public Affairs and Social Work, Detroit. 1936. 1942. Grants degree of Master of Social Work.

Western Reserve University, School of Applied Social Sciences, Cleveland. 1916. 1919. C.M. Grants degree of M.S. in Social Administration.

William and Mary, College of, Richmond School of Social Work, Richmond. 1917. 1919. C.M. Grants degree of M.S. in Social Work.

Society of New York. The school of Indiana University is very considerably cut off from its parent through being situated in Indianapolis, as is that of the College of

William and Mary in Richmond. Since field-work facilities are greater in the cities where these two schools are located than in the university towns, justification for their physical separation exists. It cannot be denied, however, that both school and university suffer from lack of closer academic relations. The National Catholic School of Social Service in Washington, D.C., is operated under the auspices of the National Council of Catholic Women. It is affiliated with, and its degrees are granted by, Catholic University, which also has its own, quite separate, school of social work. Recent cooperative undertakings between these two schools lead one to hope for eventual amalgamation.

Even when schools are located on the campus and are under immediate administrative control of the university, close relations may not exist between them and other graduate schools or undergraduate colleges. There are not a few professional schools of medicine, law, and engineering, as well as of social work, that are almost as cut off from contact with the university as they would be were they situated on an island in mid-ocean. And not infrequently where this occurs, the university has such wealth of teaching personnel, and of laboratories and libraries, as well as of special exhibits, lectures, and concerts, that the easily avoidable loss is incalculable. The problem of how all parts of the university may be more closely knit together for the benefit of teacher, student, and public has not yet yielded to solution, partly because the several schools have centered little attention upon it.

The willingness with which universities have permitted affiliation or have established new schools or departments of social work is flattering recognition of the progress which has been made by this new profession. Generally institutions of higher learning are sufficiently careful of their standards to permit a new departure in education only if they are fairly certain that the proposed subject contains a body of knowledge adequate for serious teaching—knowledge which lends itself to classification and to the development of laws governing the phenomena of the new subject.[1] The acceptance of schools of social work by the universities may be viewed as a happy achievement by those who believe, as did Mr. Frankfurter, that "the university should be the laboratory of this great new mass of scientific and social facts, and the co-ordinator of these facts for legislation, for administration, for courts, for public opinion. . . . The schools for social work must be intimate parts of the university, because they must have contact with the other branches of the university work."[2]

If many important universities are not yet offering social work courses, the reason may be attributed to other causes than an insufficient body of knowledge adaptable to scientific method and practice. Most universities are constantly cramped by lack of financial resources, and consequently develop additional curricula very slowly. Even more important than the financial problem is the frequent lack of field-work facilities. And although there is a need for many competent social workers, the demand expressed in terms of adequate salaries has not been such as to warrant the launching of graduate schools by many, if any, more universities.

[1] Hagerty, James E., "The Universities and Training for Public Leadership and Social Work," in Annals of the American Academy of Political and Social Science, vol. 105, 1923, p. 163.
[2] "Social Work and Professional Training," in Proceedings of the National Conference of Charities and Correction, 1915, p. 594.

GRADUATE TRAINING

Only a few years ago training for social work was primarily undergraduate, although some schools were operated on a strictly graduate basis. Within the decade of the 1930's, however, there was a decided shift of emphasis in favor of graduate instruction, and necessary reorganization of the curriculum went on in one school after another. This trend was in large part the result of pressure exerted by the American Association of Schools of Social Work. The Association ruled, in 1933, as will be discussed later, that no institution would after that year be considered eligible for admission to membership unless it offered at least one year of graduate work. In 1934 the Association required that all its member schools should maintain standards as high as those demanded of applicants for admission, and in 1936 it decreed that after October 1, 1939, its constituency must offer two years of graduate work. The latter ruling, however, was later modified to apply only to Type II schools.

The transition to training on an advanced level has been reflected in the marked changes that have been made in the classification of schools in this monograph since the appearance of the first edition in 1935. In that edition, which attempted to classify schools belonging to the Association with regard to graduate status, six institutions were listed as "schools admitting only college graduates."[1] Eight were classified as "primarily graduate but admitting some students without the undergraduate degree," and 15 as

[1] Those six institutions were: Graduate School of Jewish Social Work (now discontinued), and the professional schools of Bryn Mawr College, University of California, University of Pittsburgh, Smith College, and Western Reserve University.

46

"largely undergraduate, in most instances supplementing undergraduate social work courses with one or more graduate years."

When the third edition of this book was published in 1938, 23 schools out of a total of 32 were classified as offering only graduate courses. Although the other nine combined graduate with undergraduate instruction, most of them were primarily undergraduate schools. In 1942, all of the 42 schools having membership in the Association are ranked as graduate schools, and the former distinction between graduate and undergraduate institutions no longer appears in the classification. Instead, the Association's division into schools offering one year and those offering two years of graduate work is used in Table 1. Some undergraduate students, however, are admitted now, as earlier, to the graduate curricula. In November, 1941, when the total registration of 38 schools was 5,756, the number of such undergraduates, scattered among 14 schools, amounted to only 126.[1] Thus, the figure for undergraduates in graduate curricula is proportionately very small indeed.

The fact that the 42 schools are now listed as graduate, does not necessarily preclude their giving some social work courses on the undergraduate level. At the School of Social Service Administration of the University of Chicago, for example, "a carefully planned preprofessional social service program is available for students who have completed the first two years of university work and who wish to proceed directly with preparation for social service work. The two

[1] "Report on Students in Schools of Social Work, November 1, 1941," in News Letter of the American Association of Schools of Social Work, December 1, 1941, pp. 4–5.

years of the preprofessional program lead to the degree of Bachelor of Arts."[1] The bulletin states further, however, that students enrolled in the undergraduate curriculum are not permitted to take any professional courses, except Social Statistics, Child Welfare Problems, and Law and Social Work. "In particular, they are *not* allowed to take Field Work courses or any Case Work courses. For these reasons preprofessional students are not ready for positions in social work when they receive the A.B. degree. They are ready for admission to the professional program."[2]

The School of Social Administration of Ohio State University makes extensive provision for training on the undergraduate level.[3] Here also, courses in social work are offered beginning in the third college year, but before the completion of the undergraduate period the student may, as he may not at the University of Chicago, elect training in social case work and field work. Or if he prefers, he may specialize in group work and recreation, community health organization, rural social work, or social statistics. Whatever his field of specialization, he is required to do extensive work in the related social sciences. In addition to this undergraduate preparation, the school offers graduate curricula in Social Administration which are described as training "for professional positions in various fields of social work including community organization, social case work, group work and recreation, penology, research, community health organization and rural social work."[4] Hence, here is a school that provides professional education on two levels, although

---

[1] Announcements, 1941–1942, p. 13.
[2] *Ibid.*, p. 11.
[3] The Ohio State University Bulletin, April 30, 1941, pp. 28–31.
[4] *Ibid.*, p. 31.

the undergraduate work is not designated as such in its Bulletin. Only because of the graduate curricula is it permitted to hold membership in the American Association of Schools of Social Work. The school justifies its position plausibly by pointing to the existing demand for partially trained workers. The Bulletin reads, "The emphasis of the School is increasingly toward training on a graduate level. The undergraduate curricula, however, provide an excellent background for graduate work. They also equip undergraduates for the many positions, particularly in group work and case work (including probation, child welfare, and other specialized services), for which at present sufficient workers with training on a graduate level are not available."[1]

The foregoing quotation points to a situation that faces many of the universities discussed in the earlier section on Evolving Curricula of Social Work. In that discussion emphasis was centered upon efforts now being made to offer some training in areas widely separated from approved schools of social work. Toward the middle of the 1930's, however, there was such sudden need for greatly enlarged staffs in departments of public welfare that several of the state colleges and universities were urgently requested to provide training in social work. Presumably preparation on the undergraduate level would have been acceptable for many positions below the level of supervisor that the public agencies were desperately trying to fill. Ohio State University had long offered social work training, and hence was not unprepared to meet the emergency. But, in several states it looked as if a considerable number of curricula might be devised hastily, without adequate financial resources or

[1] *Ibid.*, p. 10.

49

teaching and administrative personnel, and without adequate consideration of more than temporary and local needs.

The American Association of Schools of Social Work was disturbed by the prospect of a mushroom growth that threatened standards of professional preparation that had been slowly and laboriously built up. At the same time it recognized the desirability of making some adjustment to current needs. After study by appropriate committees, it established a second form of membership in 1939, open to schools that offered not less than one year of advanced professional work, including certain specified courses, and that had at least two full-time persons as a teaching staff.[1] Such schools were to be classified as belonging to Type I, while those providing two years of acceptable graduate training were to be placed in Type II. Thus the Association set aside the rigid ruling, made earlier, that would have permitted only two-year graduate schools to be eligible for membership subsequent to 1939. Under the new plan, seven schools of Type I are now included in the national organization.[2]

REQUIREMENTS FOR ADMISSION TO SCHOOLS

One of the chief stumbling blocks in the path of an education for social work that is well rooted in a scientific background has been the hesitancy of the schools to require that their students should have had any prescribed amounts of sociology, psychology, economics, political science, anthropology, and biology. This lack of insistence has been a result of the youthfulness of professional training. In the days when schools had difficulty in attracting students, it seemed

[1] List of recommended courses appears on p. 60.
[2] See Table 1.

inadvisable for them to set up standards which would eliminate any considerable number of applicants.

More important, however, has been the unawareness of many teachers of social work of how great is the potential contribution of the social sciences to their profession. A large proportion of the faculty of the schools has been recruited, until recently, from among practicing social workers who have had no substantial grounding in the social sciences. Other teachers have been so occupied with immediate problems relating to the curriculum that they have failed to scan developments in the social studies. Still others have inferred—because of unfortunate encounters with "weak brothers" in sociology, unrealistic economists, or anthropologists whose interests run to pottery designs, kinship systems, and linguistics—that the social sciences have little to offer them. Not infrequently social workers are heard, even now, reiterating the phrase, "The contributions of the social sciences to the understanding of social forces are not yet significant."

No conclusion, in our opinion, could be fraught with more serious consequences for social work education. The social studies, certainly, are new, groping, and overburdened with small men and women. In Knowledge for What? Robert S. Lynd has castigated these studies so severely that many of their followers have not recovered from the chastisement.[1] But the same book, which deals with the place of social science in American culture, reveals that, out of the chaos, much has been learned that is indispensable for those who concern themselves with human beings.[2] In

[1] Princeton University Press, Princeton, N.J., 1939.
[2] *Ibid.*, pp. 63–114.

spite of all the inadequacies of the social studies, there emerge, at not infrequent intervals, new facts or new interpretations of fact, new theories and points of view, that are of real importance for social workers.

Few would probably question, for example, the contribution to an understanding of social forces which has been made by William Graham Sumner's Folkways, first published in 1906. Or let us turn, almost at random, to three books that have appeared within the last two years. From Professor Robert Redfield's painstaking anthropological study of the Folk Culture of Yucatan come helpful insights into the social aspects of everyday life in four widely different communities.[1] It "provides for all the rest of us," as Lynd would say, "exact data on the range of human tolerance for institutional ways different from our own."[2] In Citizens Without Work, Edward Wight Bakke, trained both in philosophy and anthropology and now professor of economics in Yale University, has set down the result of research undertaken for the purpose of discovering the problems of readjustment faced by unemployed American workers and their families and the resources which they bring with them to this task.[3] It is a study to be examined quite as much by family caseworkers as by those concerned with industrial problems and with questions of public policy. Mrs. Alva Myrdal, in Nation and Family: The Swedish Experiment in Democratic Family and Population Policy, has written a book which should be the envy of statisticians, sociologists, population experts, and social workers.[4] It is both a

[1] University of Chicago Press, Chicago, 1941.
[2] Knowledge for What? p. 157.
[3] Yale University Press, New Haven, Conn., 1940.
[4] Harper and Bros., New York, 1941.

closely reasoned argument for and a historical record of one of the most ambitious programs of social reform ever undertaken by a nation—a program in the devising of which social scientists played an essential role.

The attitude of teachers of social work toward the social sciences has been strikingly like that of teachers of law. Of late, an increasing number of legal scholars have deemed it desirable to view law not merely as a technique for regulating conduct, but as a form of social control influenced by and operating upon other social institutions. Hence, they have reached out, hoping to seize upon large segments of the social sciences ready-made to fit their immediate needs. They have inevitably been disappointed, and many have become quickly discouraged and concluded that there was little they could use. And yet at the Yale Law School, by combining economics and law, the economist, Walton Hamilton, has brought to his courses in government control of business new knowledge, theories, and ways of viewing the law, which have recently had a profound influence upon legal education and also upon political science throughout the United States.

If social work is to be more than a narrow technique, it is difficult to conceive of a type of professional training whose foundations are not laid in the social and biological sciences, since these sciences contain the basis for social work. Moreover, it is equally hard to imagine how the student can acquire adequate preparation in those schools which have built upon this subject material, unless he brings with him a rich undergraduate experience in the social studies. In recent years most schools have become increasingly aware of the existence of these two problems. After making her recent visits to the several schools holding membership in the national association, however, Professor Marion Hathway concluded:

Progress in the use of social science materials has been retarded by confusion and difference of opinion over admission requirements. While it is agreed that the student entering the professional school should be equipped with a knowledge of the social sciences, the subject-matter which constitutes this background is still a question for debate. Moreover, while social science prerequisites have been recommended by the majority of schools, the number of students still matriculating without these prerequisites is significant. Thus many of the social science offerings in the curriculum have been included to meet undergraduate deficiencies in the student background and are not primarily related to professional study.[1]

In 1937 the Curriculum Committee of the American Association of Schools of Social Work submitted certain recommendations relating to the social sciences. These recommendations, which were adopted by the Association in that year, read:

1. That economics, political science, psychology, and sociology (including social anthropology) be recognized as the preprofessional subjects most closely related to the social service curriculum.

2. That undergraduate colleges be advised to direct prospective students of social service into these departments.

3. That while a student in a school of social work should know something about each of these sciences, it is probably advisable for him to take not less than twelve semester hours or

[1] "Social Action or Inaction: the Challenge," in Training for Social Work in the Department of Social Science, University of Toronto, 1914–1940. University of Toronto Press, Toronto, 1940, p. 37.

eighteen quarter hours in one of them while doing a less amount of work in the others.

4. That the Association is unwilling at this time to designate any one of these four subjects as in general more important than any other.

5. That the Association recognizes the value to the student of courses in biology, history, and English literature and composition, and that the Association takes it for granted that students will take considerable work in these subjects.[1]

In spite of the fact that these recommendations were not only accepted by the national body but were said by their reporter, in 1937, to be "now in effect,"[2] social work education seems to have not yet come firmly to grips with the problem of what use to make of the social sciences. In the very next year it was felt by the Association that further exploration of the problem of preprofessional education was needed. The conclusions that resulted from the further exploration were not appreciably different from those of 1937, but they were much less definitely and affirmatively expressed.[3] In neither report was there evidence that effort had been made to visit social science classes or otherwise to discover the content of such courses and the effectiveness of teaching. Nor does it appear that the committees attempted to obtain the services of a well-qualified person or agency that could have devoted concentrated attention to so important a subject.

[1] "Prerequisites for Admission to Schools of Social Work: a Report of the Curriculum Committee of the American Association of Schools of Social Work," in Social Service Review, September, 1937, p. 471.

[2] Ibid., p. 471.

[3] American Association of Schools of Social Work, Committee on Pre-Social Work Education, Report on Pre-Social Work Education. Mimeographed, n.d.

Not all of the member schools have seen fit to conform to the recommendations of the Association. The New York School, which has been one of the most reluctant to publish specific admission requirements, still asks only "that the applicant shall have completed a minimum of 20 semester hours in social and biological sciences, with the emphasis in the direction of the social sciences."[1] Although many persons would agree with James E. Hagerty that "a knowledge of the structure and functions of society is as important to the social worker as physiology is to the physician,"[2] the New York School does not require a substantial course in sociology or in anthropology, either for entrance or before graduation. Six other member schools omit any reference to sociology in their admission requirements.

In spite of the fact that the form of economic organization and its degree of effectiveness determine to a very considerable extent the nature and scope of social work, 10 bulletins of schools of social work do not mention economics by name. Indifference is shown political science and government by seven schools in an era when public social work is assuming enormous proportions, and when the role of the state is being continuously enlarged. When one considers that psychiatric information is offered in all the schools, and social case work forms the basic and often most substantial part of nearly every curriculum, it is difficult to understand why nine schools currently say nothing in their catalogues about that one social science—psychology—which is centered squarely in the individual.

[1] General Announcement, 1941–1942, p. 17.
[2] "The Universities and Training for Public Leadership and Social Work," in Annals of the American Academy of Political and Social Science, vol. 105, 1923, p. 163.

Equally inexplicable is the tendency to overlook biology, including genetics and organic evolution. Yet nearly half the schools omit reference to it. There is increasing recognition that medical social workers need extensive biological knowledge, but there seems to be little general appreciation of the fact that this vital and well-developed science has a twofold contribution to make to all social workers. It can provide training in scientific method that should be of incomparable value to the social worker; it can offer demonstration of those theories of adaptation and evolution without which the nature of human society remains confused and inexplicable. No other subject has done so much, during the last three-quarters of a century, to revolutionize ideas of man, to furnish knowledge of his heritage from the past, his nature at the present, and the possibilities of his development in the future.

THE CURRICULUM

At the beginning of the twentieth century when training for social work was first making its appearance, no prepared teaching materials existed nor body of opinion about what should constitute the nature of courses offered and their content. For more than two decades professional education was experimental. As a consequence, the bulletins of the various schools exhibited confusing dissimilarity of curricula. Even within a particular school little integration of material was achieved. Many bulletins listed a number of seemingly unrelated courses. All too often subjects were chosen, not because they fitted into a professional curriculum, but because the persons teaching them happened to be interested in them or were available to the schools. As a result the student was not likely to have impressed upon him that all the processes and techniques of social work are founded on the same basic knowledge of human nature and the social environment.

In recent years much attention has been devoted to the course of study, with the result that some common pattern may be seen running through the several catalogues, while many of the individual schools have gone far in creating one or more sequences of interrelated courses. The current pattern common to the schools consists of a substantial number of courses in theory, some training in social research, and field-work instruction which, by Association ruling, may not exceed one-half of the hours devoted to theory and research.

The theoretical courses that have been most frequently offered over a considerable period are family case work, child welfare, medical social work, psychiatric social work, and community organization. Some schools financially able to provide a large number of courses have scheduled several offerings in each of these, or closely related, subjects. Other schools interested in specialization list in their bulletins a long sequence of courses in the field of specific interest, and relatively few courses in other theoretical subjects. Thus the Pennsylvania School notes training facilities in almost every variety of social case work and in several aspects of administration of social work, while Smith notes an exceptional amount of preparation in psychiatry and social psychiatric treatment.

In addition to the several courses that have had widest and longest acceptance are many that are now in process of being accepted, or that are being experimented with in a school or two. Some of these more recent additions will be discussed subsequently in considering new areas of growth in the curriculum and areas needing increased cultivation.[1]

One of the most significant occurrences in curriculum making was the adoption by the American Association of Schools of Social Work in 1932 of a minimum curriculum for the first graduate year of professional training. Prolonged labor and reconciliation of points of view were necessary before the national body accepted the plan which is presented as Table 2. Had the several schools not already made progress in examining and evaluating their own curricula, it would probably have been impossible for members of the Association to take collective action, even to the extent of determining what courses in theory should be offered in the first year. Thus adoption of the minimum curriculum may be viewed as demonstration of the fact that the schools had finally come to a willingness to accept some standards applicable to all of them.

This minimum curriculum, which has remained unchanged since 1932, has not only done much to insure a common body of knowledge in the member schools, but it has provided one of the essential criteria for deciding whether applicant schools should be found eligible for membership. During the past decade several new schools, hoping to gain membership as soon as possible, have introduced the standard curriculum immediately. Universities, furthermore, that have been unable to establish substantial schools but have initiated such social work training as they could have been greatly influenced by it.

At no time since its adoption has this curriculum been

[1] Pp. 67–89.

TABLE 2.—MINIMUM CURRICULUM ADOPTED BY THE AMERICAN
ASSOCIATION OF SCHOOLS OF SOCIAL WORK, DECEMBER, 1932[a]

1. THEORY

		Semester hours[b]	Quarter hours
Group A (all required)	Case work	2 or 3	3 or 4
	Medical information	2 or 3	3 or 4
	Psychiatric information	2 or 3	3 or 4
		Not less than 6 or more than 9	Not less than or more than 1
Group B (2 courses required)	Community organization	1, 2 or 3	2, 3 or 4
	Specialized case work	1, 2 or 3	2, 3 or 4
	Group work	1, 2 or 3	2, 3 or 4
		Not less than 4 or more than 6	Not less than or more than
Group C (2 courses required)	Field of social work	2 or 3	2, 3 or 4
	Public welfare administration	2 or 3	2, 3 or 4
	Child welfare	2 or 3	2, 3 or 4
	Problems of labor or industry	2 or 3	2, 3 or 4
		Not less than 4 or more than 6	Not less than or more than
Group D (1 course required. 2 courses may be substituted giving, in combined credit, no more than the credit allowed for one course.)	Social statistics	2 or 3	3 or 4
	Social research	2 or 3	3 or 4
	Social legislation	2 or 3	3 or 4
	Legal aspects of social work or social aspects of law	2 or 3	3 or 4
Total		20 or 22	30

2. FIELD WORK

Not more than 10 semester or 15 quarter credits of field work.

(Note: There should be not less than one semester credit or two quarter credit in any course.)

[a] This table has been reproduced with minor changes from "Progress and Problems in Soc Work Education during the Depression," by Maurice J. Karpf, in Jewish Social Service Qua terly, June, 1934, p. 259.
[b] Figures appearing under "semester hours" indicate the amount of classroom time per we recommended for the various courses during one semester—one-half an academic year. Figur under "quarter hours" are applicable to schools which divide their academic year into th quarters (or four quarters if there is a summer session).

considered altogether satisfactory. Some of the early critics maintained that the subject matter included in medical and psychiatric information did not warrant recognition by a graduate professional school. Others felt that the proposed course of study included too wide an area of unrelated subject matter. Still others wished for greater flexibility by the addition of further electives to Groups C and D. As a result of the changes that have been sweeping over social work in recent years and also as a result of the recent extensive study by the Association, Education for the Public Social Services,[1] there has been increasing awareness that the curriculum, unamended during a decade, must now undergo alteration. Hence the Curriculum Committee of the Association is currently attempting to decide what changes should be made, and subcommittees have been charged with outlining the material that should be included in the proposed courses, preparatory to action by the Association.

As yet discussion and agreement have not proceeded far enough to result in official action.[2] It can be said, however, that members of the subcommittee considering public welfare are agreed that at least one course in that subject should be required of all students. Because of the importance that group work is assuming, the appropriate subcommittee has concluded that a basic course in the subject should also be required by every school as soon as well-qualified instructors can be added to the faculties. Case work and field work, furthermore, will unquestionably continue to be required, as in the past, of all students.

[1] University of North Carolina Press, Chapel Hill, 1942.
[2] American Association of Schools of Social Work, Meeting of the Curriculum Committee, November 14–15, 1941, Chicago. Mimeographed, n.d.

Field work, which constitutes an important part of the curriculum of all schools, is planned and supervised experience in the practice of social work, as currently carried on by recognized social agencies, to which students are assigned. It corresponds in purpose to the clinical teaching of medical schools. The emphasis which is placed upon it and the efficiency with which it is pursued differ widely from institution to institution. The type and amount, as planned by any one school, depend upon the educational standards of that school, the proximity to appropriate agencies, the kind of supervision which is available, and the philosophy of the school regarding its purpose and significance.

Field-work teaching was begun in the offices of the family welfare societies. It has been extended to such organizations as children's agencies and institutions, child guidance clinics, juvenile courts, medical social work departments of hospitals and clinics including hospitals for the mentally ill, visiting teacher service of the public schools, bureaus for home relief or general assistance and other departments of public welfare agencies, group-work agencies, councils of social agencies, and even some agencies promoting social action. In some schools the student is expected to begin his field-work experience in a family welfare society, in order to profit from its broad generalized program before going on to the more specialized types of social case work or to other forms of social work. Recently several schools have assigned students to departments of public welfare for initial field work, and there is a general growing tendency to provide at least some training in public social service agencies.

By ruling of the national association, field work must be under the educational direction of the school rather than the agency that provides the clinical facilities.[1] Immediate supervision, however, is obtained in various ways. An increasing number of schools include field-work supervision among the duties of faculty members. Instructors, who have themselves had training and experience in social work practice, are assigned to the offices of the co-operating agencies during the period when students are there. These instructors have no responsibility for carrying any part of the caseload of the agencies; their time belongs exclusively to the students. Some schools pay part of the salary of a staff member in the agency providing the field work, who guides and instructs their students. Still other schools have entered into co-operative relations with selected agencies which assume responsibility for both cost of and instruction in field work.

It is generally recognized that the philosophy and practice of field work have undergone and are still undergoing radical and desirable change. Until the last decade field work represented the most substantial training offered in some of the schools, where it occupied up to 80 per cent of the scheduled hours.[2] The emphasis placed upon it was the result, partly, of the paucity of prepared teaching materials for courses in theory, and partly, of the conviction that students should be so thoroughly acquainted with social work practice that they would be able to fill positions of responsibility immediately after leaving the school. This point of view is now rarely expressed.

The emphasis placed upon field work today stems from

[1] American Association of Schools of Social Work, Constitution and By-Laws, sec. 2.

[2] Karpf, Maurice J., The Scientific Basis of Social Work. Columbia University Press, New York, 1931, p. 334.

realization that the decisions which social case work requires can be safely made only after supervised experience in the actual treatment of cases, under able teachers, in centers where care is being given regularly to clients. Since responsibilities that must be borne by the social worker relate so closely to the welfare of individual human beings, they cannot be entrusted to persons who have not themselves carried minor case-work responsibilities under competent and experienced instructors.[1] Porter R. Lee and Marion E. Kenworthy defined the distinctive function of field work as follows:

1. To provide an opportunity for the development of skill through practice in the use of its several ingredients: knowledge, philosophy, and technique.

2. To develop in students the ability to discern in actual situations and in human beings facts and concepts with which they have become intellectually familiar through study.

3. To provide the test of practicality for theories and methods with which students have become familiar through study.[2]

Research constitutes another division of the curriculum of social work schools. Nearly every bulletin notes one and generally two or more courses in some aspect of research. The University of Chicago, for instance, lists a considerable number of courses, and Ohio State and Pittsburgh also have extensive offerings. Social statistics appears most frequently as the subject to which attention is devoted. It can be assumed, moreover, that statistical method is also taught in some of the courses designated by the general title, Methods

---

[1] Abbott, Edith, "Education for Social Work," in Social Work Year Book, 1933, p. 146.

[2] Mental Hygiene and Social Work. The Commonwealth Fund, New York, 1931, p. 184.

of Social Research. Important as are statistics, the fact must be stressed that they provide only one research procedure. For some inexplicable reason American educational and research institutions are now, in our opinion, overemphasizing this subject at the expense of training in and use of other methods. And schools of social work seem to have fallen into the same error.

It is the students now in schools of social work who will supposedly be obliged in future years, not merely to maintain the status quo of the profession, but to gather and interpret new data and formulate new plans and policies. The adaptation of existing principles and methods to changing needs and the creation of fresh techniques to meet emergent situations are tasks of such magnitude that the prospective social worker needs all the preparation that can be given him. Particularly important is it that he gain acquaintance with sociological and anthropological methods of collecting, analyzing, and presenting new material, such, for example, as those utilized in the two studies of Middletown,[1] in the social examination of Pittsburgh,[2] and in the recent report of several anthropologists entitled, Deep South.[3]

At a time when the need for wider general knowledge of social conditions is being increasingly recognized, the responsibility of the schools for promotion of journalistic writing could also be profitably considered. Martha Gellhorn's The Trouble I've Seen,[4] Carey McWilliams' Fac-

[1] Lynd, Robert S., and Lynd, Helen Merrell, Middletown and Middletown in Transition. Harcourt, Brace and Co., New York, 1929 and 1937.
[2] Klein, Philip, A Social Study of Pittsburgh.
[3] Directed by W. L. Warner, Allison Davis, and others. University of Chicago Press, Chicago, 1941.
[4] William Morrow and Co., New York, 1936.

tories in the Fields: the Story of Migratory Farm Labor in California,[1] and America's Own Refugees: Our 4,000,000 Homeless Migrants, by Henry Hill Collins,[2] are illustrative of books designed to reach the reading public that should be published in far greater numbers. No group is in better position than are social workers to know the basic facts about which such books are written. Schools of social work could do much, through their faculties and through encouragement of prospective social workers, to recruit professional writers to whom necessary source materials would be made available.

This last suggestion leads to consideration of the obligation of faculties for carrying on research as well as for teaching methods of research to students. It has been widely assumed that institutions of higher learning have two functions, the second of which is scholarly research and publication. It can scarcely be said that schools of social work have, as yet, made this second function a general and conscious part of their program. In their early days they were handicapped by a philosophy of action rather than of reflection. This is true to only a lesser degree now. They have been beset on the one hand by many problems incident to their "newness" and to the lack of financial support, and on the other by the backwardness of the agencies in understanding what constitutes professional education. Hence they have often lost perspective.

In a few schools the faculties are doing a considerable amount of research. The total publications within a year of all the schools, however, probably do not exceed those of

[1] Little, Brown and Co., Boston, 1939.
[2] Princeton University Press, Princeton, N.J., 1941.

the departments of social science of any one of several universities that might be mentioned. They are still entirely inadequate to provide more than a small fraction of the subject matter seriously needed for instruction. Although great quantities of records are on file in agencies, they have not been made as extensively available for use as have the records of medical and legal cases. When professorial chairs are established in schools of social work, it is of vital importance that opportunity for investigation and publication be clearly provided, and every encouragement be offered for the advancement of scholarship.

NEW AREAS OF GROWTH IN THE CURRICULUM

Thus far the discussion has concerned itself with portions of the curriculum that have become most nearly standardized as a result of the cultivation of years and the action of the American Association of Schools of Social Work. In the meantime, however, public social work has not only undergone great augmentation, but the social philosophy of the era has found expression in enlarged legislative efforts that have important implications for social work. Has professional training reflected these rapid changes? This is a question that needs more authoritative answer than has been accorded it. Hence some attention will be devoted to a survey of new areas of growth within the curricula of schools of social work.

Particularly noticeable has been the introduction of elements of law and of legal materials in the schools. Although medical and psychiatric information have long been required by the national association, legal information has been required only as one of four alternatives, and many schools made no effort until recently to provide instruction in it. Now, at least 30 of the 39 schools belonging to the Association in February, 1942,[1] give a course which most often appears as Social Work and the Law, Legal Aspects of Social Work, or Law and Social Work. A few schools offer further specialized information in such a subject as Legal Protection of the Child. The University of Chicago, which has cultivated this field longer and more intensively than has any other school, announced in a recent bulletin the following courses: Law and Social Work, Child and the State, Courts and Social Work, Family and the State, Legal Aspects of Family Problems.[2]

Courses such as the above concern themselves with those portions of the common and statutory law which social workers need to know if they are to recognize legal problems and if they are to advise clients wisely. But there are other areas where law is being reflected in social work education. All public social work is the creation of legislation and of administrative rulings. Hence it is essential that administrators of public assistance and public welfare programs, as well as others responsible for the determination of public policy, be conversant with the legal framework within which such agencies operate. As a consequence statutory provisions and their interpretation occupy a considerable place in courses in public welfare administration, which have sprung up in a large majority of the schools during the last decade.

[1] Bulletins of member schools were consulted before the admission of three additional institutions in May, 1942. Hence figures appearing in this and subsequent sections apply to only the 39 institutions that constituted the Association as of February, 1942.

[2] The School of Social Service Administration, Announcements, May 25, 1941, pp. 27–28.

It should be noted parenthetically that increased attention is also being given to the function of administration of social agencies, public and private. Some 25 schools now offer one and sometimes more courses, most commonly entitled, Administration of Social Agencies. Law plays small part in them. Rather do they reflect the growing realization in America that administration is, in itself, a subject of importance, and the quickened awareness of social work agencies that their effectiveness is dependent, to no inconsiderable degree, upon the extent to which they can perfect the administrative process.

In social legislation and in social insurance, emphasis is placed upon statutory materials. These courses, in purpose and selection of data, probably vary widely from school to school. In some institutions they are designed to give the student general knowledge of significant methods of attempting to solve problems that arise most frequently from economic insecurity. In other institutions they are presented, not for the purpose of broad orientation, but rather as technical courses which concentrate attention upon specific statutory provisions and their implementation through administrative rulings. Regardless of content, the important fact cannot be disregarded that 22 schools offered, in a recent year, at least one course in social insurance. The University of Chicago offered four. Nine schools also offered instruction in the broader field of social legislation. In at least three instances, this instruction was given by a teacher trained in law as well as in social work.

Courses in law and social work, administration of public welfare, administration of social agencies, and social insurance have now found a real place for themselves within the schools of social work. So have courses in group work. Recent bulletins indicate that at least 34 approved schools provide one or more such courses. Atlanta, Boston University, Carnegie, Indiana, National Catholic, New York, Ohio State, Pittsburgh, and Western Reserve have built up extensive offerings. Besides schools having membership in the Association, Temple University maintains a department devoted exclusively to social group work; George Williams College in Chicago trains increasing numbers of graduate students for positions in group-work agencies; and several colleges provide preparation largely on the undergraduate level for positions in the Y.M.C.A. and in church group work.[1]

This growth is somewhat phenomenal since "group work as a consciously defined method is a comparatively new development in education, recreation, and social work."[2] Many agencies had built their entire programs upon a foundation of group organization and group leadership long before there was common recognition of group work as a generic concept. In recent years social work, as well as education and recreation, has come increasingly to see the value of employing a type of educational process carried on in voluntary groups during leisure time with the assistance of a group leader. It conceives of group work as a method that emphasizes the role of the group *as* education as well as *in* education, and that provides creative experience which serves social ends. On the basis of this theory schools of social work have not only introduced the courses noted, but

[1] See statements concerning schools that offer training for the Y.M.C.A. and church social work in the Appendix, pp. 212–216.

[2] For a brief description of social group work, see Hendry, Charles E., "Social Group Work," in Social Work Year Book, 1941, pp. 523–530.

much attention is now being devoted to further examination of what should constitute the content of professional education in this field.

One other subject has attracted general interest. It is that of industrial relations or labor problems. Examination of bulletins showed that at least 24 of the approved schools gave, or made provision elsewhere in the university for, a total of 34 such courses. Thanks to the productive years of study that John A. Fitch has devoted to the subject, the New York School was able to offer courses in Industrial Relations, Labor Problems and Social Work, and Current Industrial Problems. Bryn Mawr scheduled a course in European Labour Movements as well as one in American Labour Movements; Fordham students received instruction from a distinguished law-trained professor of economics who had been the executive officer of the German Labor Administration under the Weimar Republic; Chicago offered, for its summer session, courses in Trade Unions, Collective Bargaining and Industrial Arbitration, and the State in Relation to Labor.

Another area in which rate of growth has been rapid, although less dispersion has been achieved, is that of training for supervision in social work. Seventeen schools noted one or more courses. Although the majority of these courses were probably most concerned with supervision of casework practice, seven were designated as supervision in group work. Six were offered exclusively to employed social workers.

Fourteen schools considered public health sufficiently important to offer a course in it. The University of California obtained the services of Dr. C.-E. A. Winslow of the Yale

Medical School for a limited time to discuss Public Health as a Social Program, and Health Problems of Defense and Post-War Reconstruction. At the New York School Dr. Franz Goldmann, also of Yale, presented in the current academic year a highly popular course on basic economic and social concepts of health services. Loyola listed not only Public Health for Social Workers but Health Insurance. Several schools, through their bulletins, registered interest in such insurance and in a greatly enlarged national health program.

Housing appeared to be the next subject to which the schools had turned. Nine listed courses under some such name as Social Aspects of Housing, Public Housing and Community Planning, or Low Rent Housing. The University of Washington listed Housing Management. The Atlanta School appeared to be in one of the most advantageous positions to offer work in this field. University Homes and John Hope Homes, two low-cost housing projects, are adjacent to the campus of the University. The instructor of the course, Alonzo G. Moron, is housing manager of these two units. This school reported that it placed no fewer than 11 of its graduates in one year in positions as tenant investigators, senior investigators, or supervisors of tenant selection for the housing authorities of Atlanta, Charlotte, Chattanooga, Chicago, Louisville, and New Orleans.[1]

AREAS NEEDING INCREASED CULTIVATION

In contrast to the encouraging initiation of some training in the subjects just enumerated, progress has been disap-

[1] Atlanta University School of Social Work, Bulletin, 1940–1941, pp. 19–21.

pointingly small in several other important areas. Few opportunities exist to obtain specific knowledge of economic and psychological conditions under which rural social work must be done, or of the various ethnic groups who provide a large proportion of urban clients. Although courses in the historical and legislative aspects of social insurance are not now infrequent, training for practice in agencies administering unemployment compensation and employment service and old-age insurance is almost non-existent. More unfortunate is the lack of emphasis placed upon training for the administrative level and for planning and formulation of policies of social work.

1. *Rural Social Work*

Social work is still relatively unorganized in rural sections, but significant developments of the last thirty years point to a rapidly increasing awareness of the need for amelioration of social and economic problems of country life.[1] Federal programs illustrate how dynamic has been the interest and how great the area of growth in assisting rural people. They also indicate the expanding scope of rural social work, which has often been made an integral part of a broad plan of rehabilitation. The Extension Service of the United States Department of Agriculture and that of the state colleges of agriculture have administered co-operatively, since 1914, the most widespread rural program in the nation. Through its vast plan of relief, rehabilitation, and resettlement, the Farm Security Administration has been,

[1] See Landis, Benson Y., "Rural Social Programs," in Social Work Year Book, 1941, pp. 490–498.

subsequent to 1935, the spearhead of national relief efforts among farm families. To its Regional and County Family Service, in particular, have been appointed many social workers. Authority has been reposed in the Children's Bureau to apportion funds for rural child welfare, crippled children, and maternal and child health; in the United States Public Health Service, for the creation and support of county departments of public health. The Tennessee Valley Authority, the Civilian Conservation Corps, the Work Projects Administration, and other federal agencies have also contributed services extensively to rural areas.

In spite of this manifest concern about the welfare of some 57,000,000 persons who now live on farms or in villages of less than 2,500 population, scarcely more than one-third of the approved schools make any provision for courses in rural social work or in rural social and economic conditions. Of the schools under private auspices only Simmons, Catholic University, Atlanta, Western Reserve, Chicago, and the two in St. Louis occupy themselves with the subject. State universities, surprisingly enough, seem to do no better. Five list courses in Rural Social Work or Public Welfare Administration in Rural Areas, one of which is a preprofessional course. The University of North Carolina notes that in Community Organization for Social Work and Social Work Administration emphasis is placed upon applicability to rural and small-town areas. In courses in administration in the schools of other states which are predominantly rural, it is likely that similar emphasis occurs. When a specific subject is interpolated into such a course as administration, however, the attention it will receive is dependent upon the interest and experience of the instructor

74

and the manner in which he organizes the material of the course.

It must be recalled, moreover, that what the social worker probably needs most as background for practice in rural areas is an intimate knowledge of those sociological and psychological ways of thinking and behaving that manifest themselves in non-urban places; of the educational and community resources that both reflect and determine standards of living and cultural levels; of economic forces which have produced the sharecropper, tenant farmer, and migrant, and also large-scale, mechanized farming and the Associated Farmers. Such knowledge will rarely be provided except through substantial courses designed expressly for the purpose.

The question of preparation for rural social work has received much attention in recent years. There has been sharp criticism of the frequent inability of urban workers to make effective adjustment to rural conditions, and equally sharp criticism of the failure of the schools to prepare students for rural practice. Establishment of graduate schools within land-grant colleges has been recommended—and a few have been opened—on the assumption that such colleges not only understand rural life, but are already furnishing statewide aid and leadership through their extension services and their experiment stations.[1] In its report on Education for the Public Social Services, the study committee of the American Association of Schools of Social Work pointed to the unsatisfactory current situation. It expressed belief, however, that

[1] "Report of the Joint Committee on Accrediting Representing the Land-Grant Colleges and State Universities," in Proceedings of the Association of Land-Grant Colleges and Universities, 1938, pp. 330–333.

differences between rural and urban practice resulted largely from differences of culture patterns, and maintained that skills and knowledge basic to one type of practice were basic to the other.[1] The entire question of preparation for rural social work is now the subject of inquiry by a special committee of the Association.

2. *Ethnic Problems*

Courses devoted to examination of the problems encountered by the foreign born and by the several minority groups are even fewer in number than are those relating to rural social work. As might be expected, the Atlanta School orientates its entire program toward social work for Negroes. Forrester Washington's course, Social Work among Negroes in America, provides concentrated discussion of the political, economic, and social factors which make for Negro maladjustment, and of various attempted solutions.[2] Because of the invaluable experience of Mary Hurlbutt, the New York School probably offers the richest insight of any school into the ethnic problems of diverse groups. The family life of transplanted Europeans and their American children is considered in one of her courses; in another, each student is given opportunity to study an ethnic group in New York City; a third course deals with technical problems of aliens. Chicago devotes one course and part of another to the economic and cultural adjustments required of immigrants, and to legislation concerning immigration and naturalization. Only three other schools appear to offer so much as one such course on the graduate level. At the school of

[1] University of North Carolina Press, Chapel Hill, 1942, pp. 217–218.
[2] Atlanta University School of Social Work, Bulletin, 1940–1941, pp. 63–64.

William and Mary, the course on Races and Ethnic Groups directs particular attention to relations between Negroes and whites. Western Reserve is concerned both with Negroes and with immigrants, while the University of Denver, in Minority Population Groups, centers attention on Mexican, Spaniard, American Indian, and Negro.

The federal census of 1940 showed a total of 11,400,000 foreign-born white persons in continental United States. In addition, there were almost 13,000,000 Negroes, an undetermined number of Puerto Ricans, 300,000 American Indians, and a quarter of a million members of the brown and yellow races. Twenty-eight per cent of the population of New York City was composed of foreign-born whites, not including Puerto Ricans, and 6 per cent of Negroes. In Boston 24 per cent were foreign-born whites and 3 per cent were Negroes. The percentage of white persons born in other countries was 20 in Chicago, Cleveland, Detroit, and San Francisco. Negroes constituted from 8 to 10 per cent of the population in the first three of these four cities; in San Francisco, less than 1 per cent.

Large as are these figures, a decrease of 2,500,000 foreign-born whites resulted, between 1930 and 1940, from the exceptionally heavy emigration of the early 1930's, and from the high mortality of the increasing proportion of the foreign born who are now in the older age groups. Regardless of this decrease, a disproportionately large amount of urban social work must necessarily continue for some years to be devoted to the foreign born and to their children, who, though citizens of the United States, continue to experience many hardships. Extensive social work is now urgently needed for such racial groups as Negroes, Indians, Puerto

77

Ricans, Mexicans, and Japanese.[1] And yet, except at Atlanta, no preparation is required for understanding the peculiar problems presented by those who have migrated to the United States or who are obliged to live under distinct political, social, and economic disadvantages. Sufficient reliance cannot be placed upon introducing relevant data in the various case- and group-work courses, for what the student most needs is the cultivation of understanding, profound interest in, and liking for persons born into a different culture. Hence, unless the schools should see fit to prescribe for admission a certain amount of work in pertinent anthropological and sociological courses, it would seem of primary importance that at least one substantial course in ethnic groups and their problems be offered to every social work student.

3. *Unemployment Compensation and Employment Service, and Old-Age Insurance*

In 1933 a system of grants-in-aid to the several states was established by federal statute for the operation of state employment offices. The Social Security Act of 1935 made provision for a payroll tax on designated industries, 90 per cent of which was to be returned to those states enacting unemployment compensation laws that included certain minimum standards. Thus were created parallel services for the purpose of helping the unemployed to find jobs and of providing them with some compensation during a limited pe-

[1] Since the above statement was written, the resettlement of some 70,000 American citizens of Japanese descent and 40,000 Japanese aliens formerly living chiefly on the West Coast has presented social workers, as well as others interested in social welfare and civil liberties, with a most challenging problem.

riod of unemployment. Since 1937 they have been integrated administratively in Washington, and are now administered by the Bureau of Employment Security of the Social Security Board. Recently all state control has been removed from the employment offices, which will be federally operated for at least the duration of the war.

So vast are these services that on May 1, 1939, they employed, so it has been reported, more than 36,000 persons.[1] Fifty-seven per cent were in unemployment compensation, and 43 per cent in the employment service. Only rough figures can be given for the size of the personnel on the various levels. "Data from the employment service covering principally the third quarter of 1939 . . . indicate that 276 were classified as state administrative [personnel], 934 as local administrative, 2,531 as senior interviewers, and 4,534 as junior interviewers. It is not possible to obtain figures for the classification of state unemployment compensation services, but it is estimated that between 5 and 15 per cent would fall in the operating, supervisory, or administrative levels and the balance in clerical personnel. The fact that the personnel in the two services is interchangeable in many administrations . . . minimizes the usefulness of these estimates."[2] In addition to the large number of persons employed by the states or in local offices, the federal office of the Bureau of Employment Security had, on June 30, 1940, a staff of 790, of whom 610 were classified as "departmental" and 180 as "field."[3]

[1] American Association of Schools of Social Work, Education for the Public Social Services, p. 56.
[2] Ibid.
[3] Federal Security Agency, Fifth Annual Report of the Social Security Board, 1940. Government Printing Office, Washington, 1941, p. 160.

The Social Security Act of 1935 also made provision for a system of old-age insurance, the benefits of which should become available to workers in covered industries upon reaching sixty-five years of age. By amendment to the Act in 1939, survivors' benefits were added, and the revised program became known as Old-Age and Survivors Insurance. It is federally financed, and is operated by the Bureau of Old-Age and Survivors Insurance of the Social Security Board. In February, 1939, the 327 offices in the several states employed 1,643 persons of whom 309 were managers, 152 were assistant managers, and the remainder were claims interviewers, personnel clerks, and typists. Since that time the number of offices, and hence of personnel, has been greatly increased.[1] In June, 1940, employes of the Bureau alone were reported to be in excess of 8,900. Four thousand nine hundred were classified as "departmental," nearly 4,000 as "field." A considerable proportion of these employes, however, were engaged exclusively in accounting operations.

Offices administering unemployment compensation and employment service, and old-age and survivors insurance are not often considered social work agencies, and their technical positions were not listed under social work titles by the Bureau of the Census when preparing for the census of 1940. However, some social workers are employed in them. A recent examination of these offices, furthermore, convinced the Study Committee of the American Association of Schools of Social Work that specific services, offered to individual clients and involving discretionary action, rest on a

---

[1] American Association of Schools of Social Work, Education for the Public Social Services, pp. 53–54.

foundation of knowledge and skills for which social work training would be highly desirable.[1] After a job analysis of the operating, administrative, and supervisory levels of these services and also of public assistance and public child welfare, the Committee concluded:

The nature of the jobs established in the services studied demands the knowledge and skills of social work and indicates the need for professional education at the graduate level. . . . In public assistance and in child welfare, complete professional preparation is accepted as essential, in spite of the fact that such requirement cannot be imposed at the present time. In old age insurance, unemployment compensation and the employment service ultimate justification of such requirement is based upon the recognition of the needs inherent in the job. . . .

Although the study revealed certain common elements of preparation needed by the personnel, these have not been recognized by the separate services, and variations in personnel requirements accordingly hinder selection of qualified people. In all the services reviewed, however, there is a trend towards establishing higher pre-entry standards for technical positions. Among the services studied, old age insurance is giving most attention to outlining promotional possibilities and to other progressive personnel policies. This service has not given equal attention, however, to the content of the job as related to education. In unemployment compensation and the employment service, a certain minimum of paid experience is required of all applicants for appointment at any level. Because of this requirement, graduates of colleges or professional schools without paid work experience are not eligible to the entering job level in these programs. . . . So far as old age insurance and unemployment compensation and the employment service are concerned, the schools [of social work] have made no significant effort to offer preparation for these new forms of public administration. A partial explanation,

[1] *Ibid.,* p. 12.

however, is the lack of encouragement to the schools by these services.[1]

Verification of the statement that the schools have made no significant effort to offer training is afforded by the bulletins. Each of three schools noted one course on the Public Employment Service, but that offered by Oklahoma was on the undergraduate level. Loyola listed two courses: one, an international comparison of public employment services; the other, Unemployment Compensation. Under the title, Treatment and Prevention of Unemployment, Indiana included consideration of unemployment insurance and employment service. Five schools made some small provision for work in vocational guidance and placement, or in techniques of counseling. Seven offered, or referred students to, a course in mental testing. Most of these latter courses, however, were not designed primarily to aid the social worker with vocational counseling and placement.

In spite of the valuable initial contribution made by the Association of Schools through its investigation of the public services, two essential questions await further exploration. The first is that of the extent to which these offices would consider it desirable to utilize social workers. The second is the question of what would constitute the most effective preparation of students, were the schools to have some assurance that a demand for their graduates existed. The first can, perhaps, be answered only after prolonged cultivation of discussion between the services and the schools. And if the schools should decide to extend their training, they would need advice in planning the curriculum from those responsible for the formulation of policies for these offices.

[1] *Ibid.,* pp. 14, 15, 17–18.

4. *Administration and Planning of Social Work*

Schools of social work have been primarily engaged in the training of persons for "line" positions, and they have also offered some preparation to active or prospective supervisors of case and of group work. They have made relatively slight provision for the professional education of persons who must act as executive officers of social work agencies, or who must formulate policies for professional associations, social work councils, federal and state planning and administrative agencies, and organizations primarily concerned with social action. As a consequence, the criticism has been made that their graduates cannot assume responsibility for executive and research work as readily as do graduates of schools of public administration and of law.

Reference has already been made to the fact that the majority of the schools have now introduced one or more courses in public welfare administration and the administration of social agencies. These courses are undoubtedly of real assistance to persons who subsequently find themselves in executive positions, as is much material that can be gleaned from courses relating to public welfare programs and community organization. Except at Chicago and to a lesser extent at two or three other schools, however, courses in administration are few in number and elementary in nature. Evidence of the paucity of specialized work in administration and planning appears in the bulletins issued by the schools. So important a subject as the financial administration of either public or private welfare received special attention in a recent year only in nine schools. In probably half of the courses listed, the discussion was directed exclusively to the financing of the public social services. Seven schools set down a course in personnel administration; in four instances it was designated as dealing with public welfare personnel.

In the field of social work interpretation or public relations, eight schools listed one course, and the New York School two. Half of these had made their appearance within very recent years. In courses in community organization or community relations some reference is probably made to the importance of the interpretation of social work to the public. As is the case with all these specialized subjects, however, lack of time in the broad general course prevents more than rudimentary analysis of method.

Examination of bulletins in reference to training for work in professional associations, councils, and administrative agencies revealed that Boston College offered a course in Administration of Chests and Councils, while Ohio State offered two courses—the Community Chest Movement, and National Social Work Agencies and Local Programs. For the preparation of teachers of social work, only Pennsylvania and New York noted any provision whatever.

For purposes of contrast, we should like to refer to two curricula, not specifically in social work but in the closely related area of training for public administration. The first was offered in 1941–1942 by the Graduate Division for Training in Public Service of New York University; the second, in the same year, by the Graduate School of Public Affairs of American University in Washington, D.C. At New York University the curriculum was designed almost exclusively for persons who occupy or will occupy supervisory, executive, or research positions in governmental agencies, and it included preparation for the administration of public welfare agencies and institutions. The following main categories under which the various courses were grouped indicate the scope of the curriculum and the extent to which emphasis was placed upon the administrative process. Only courses in statistics and accounting, which were taught as specific techniques, have any appearance of being outside the field of administration and planning.

Public Administration
Public Financial Administration
Public-Health Administration
Public Personnel Administration
Welfare Administration
Public Planning
Housing Management
Statistics and Accounting
Social Security Administration
Labor-Law Administration
Administrative Law

The Graduate School of Public Affairs of American University offers advanced education in the theoretical and applied aspects of the social sciences. Both faculty and student body are drawn largely from the federal services. The exceptional facilities, available to the school because of its situation in Washington, make possible a wealth of courses. In turn, it strives to enrich not only the federal but other public and quasi-public services. Certain portions of its curriculum are of especial interest to social workers. Within the sequence of courses in Social Economy, offered in 1941–1942, was a group of courses entitled Social Security and Social Welfare that included the following:

Principles of Social Security in the United States and Abroad
Current Issues in Social Security
Administrative Problems in Labor Legislation and Social Security
Social and Economic Aspects of Health and Medical Care
Economic and Social Problems of Housing
Land, Housing, and Planning Problems in American Cities
Labor Market Policy and Labor Market Administration
Seminar in Social Security

Within the sequence in Political Science and Public Administration were courses in:

Financial Administration
Organization and Management of Public Offices
Public Personnel Management
Public Relations

Under Economics were listed:

Labor Economics
Agricultural Economics and National Resources
Social Control and Economic Planning

When the curricula of the schools of social work are placed side by side with the curricula of these and other schools for training in public service, one is likely to conclude that professional preparation available for the higher levels of social work is more meager than had been realized. Social workers have consistently maintained that case-work training is basic for all other professional preparation and that a foundation in the principles of case work is needed even for the administration of social work agencies, whether private or public. So intent has been adherence to this point of view and so desirous have been the schools to perfect the content of courses in case work, that there seem to have been insufficient time and perspective for developing other essential areas of the curriculum.

That case work is a technique of real importance is un-challenged. Individualization of treatment represents one of the great advances in social welfare and social justice. But some schools have so elaborated the case-work method that their catalogues are as overweighted with such courses as are those of certain law schools that devote almost exclusive attention to the study of cases—presented in the form of judicial opinions—in an era when legal control is rapidly passing from the judge to the legislator and the administrative agency.

Schools of social work, furthermore, appear to have overlooked the fact that the number of positions in the field of social work that are far removed from case work or group practice is already large. If this country continues a controlled economy, even to the extent to which the trend prior to this war pointed, and if social workers assume their appropriate share of responsibility for improving the environment in which people live, the number of such positions will greatly increase. Were a census to be taken of those persons now employed by the federal government, by the states and local communities, and by private organizations and foundations in programs of research, planning, and formulation of public policy, the count would probably be surprising. The schools and the professional associations of social work seem to be scarcely more aware of the implications of this growth than was recently a distinguished law school dean who had not realized that there were already many opportunities in the public service for his graduates. When a census, in 1939, revealed that there were more than 5,000 lawyers in the federal employ alone, he concluded that training for and placement in the public service were matters warranting the immediate attention of his school.

If society is to be effectively served, schools of social work must, in our opinion, either offer a much expanded and enriched curriculum or they must recognize the validity of other curricula as training for the large and increasing number of administrative and planning positions in public welfare. With adequate financial support and competent faculties, courses constructed on a foundation of the social sciences, including law, and designed for the higher levels of social work could readily be built into the schools. In the recruiting of faculties for such purposes, it should be borne in mind that there are now in this country large numbers of European scholars with long experience in administration and research who would provide an invaluable source of supply and whose services have scarcely been tapped by the schools. The New School for Social Research in New York City has demonstrated how great a contribution such persons can make, and has incidentally gained great additional prestige for itself.

Should the schools find it impossible for them to strengthen this area of training in the near future, it would seem essential that efforts be made to establish co-operative relations with graduate departments of public administration and of the social sciences. Here the Committee on Public Administration of the Social Science Research Council, interested in cultivation of training for all public service and in strengthening the bonds between existing curricula, would willingly lend valuable advice and assistance. Many persons occupying important social work positions have received their training exclusively in other departments than those of social work. Now, when there is increasing recognition of the desirability of greater knowledge on the part of social workers of political science, law, economics, sociology, and psychology, as well as of the administrative process, we believe that the schools should thoroughly canvass the possibility of using existing facilities within their universities. Many of the graduate courses certainly can offer social work students little. But we believe it safe to predict that many schools would discover a surprisingly large number of instructors in other departments to whom students might profitably be entrusted.

NUMBER OF STUDENTS AND OF GRADUATES

The total number of students of social work is not known. Each year, however, the American Association of Schools of Social Work collects statistics of those enrolled in its member schools as of November 1, and also of those enrolled during any portion of the preceding academic year. The relatively large number of students who attend a school of social work for only part of the academic year greatly increases the total figure for the year. Thus, 38 Association schools reported 5,047 students majoring in social work on November 1, 1940, but a total of 7,425 for the entire academic year, including the summer session, of 1940–1941.

Table 3, showing the November enrollment in 1941, has been prepared from the most recent report of the Association. Certain interesting considerations emerge from these and supplementary figures. It will be noted, first, that nearly 20 per cent of the students of November, 1941, were men.

The percentage in 1936 had been 17. Although certain types of social work are still carried on predominantly by women, expansion of public social work and of group work has attracted an increasing proportion of men. This increase is reflected in the slowly rising percentage of men who attend schools of social work. It is still true, however,

TABLE 3.—STUDENTS MAJORING IN SOCIAL WORK IN 38
ASSOCIATION SCHOOLS, NOVEMBER 1, 1941, BY SEX
AND FULL- OR PART-TIME STATUS

	Men	Women	Total
Full-time	494	2,030	2,524
Part-time	460	1,902	2,362
Total	954	3,932	4,886
Per cent	19.5	80.5	100

that many men enter the profession with other kinds of training, such as that in business administration, public administration, law, or advanced academic work in the social sciences.

The table shows, secondly, that a little more than half of the students electing the regular curriculum were registered for full-time work. Prior to 1934, when full-time students first exceeded those doing part-time work, a considerable majority had matriculated in only a few courses a semester. Although during three of the seven subsequent years the record of 1934 has not been maintained, the trend is in the direction of enrollment on a full-time basis.

Table 4 presents supplementary information about the number of students in November, 1941, in each of the 38 member schools of that year.

TABLE 4.—ENROLLMENT IN INDIVIDUAL ASSOCIATION
SCHOOLS, NOVEMBER 1, 1941[a]

(Schools in order of total number of students)

| School | Number of students | | |
	Total	Full-time	Part-time
More than 200 students			
New York	850	278	572
Chicago	546	336	210
Western Reserve	332	170	162
Pennsylvania	209	104	105
Washington University	205	70	135
Between 100 and 200 students			
Tulane	190	99	91
Pittsburgh	164	87	77
Minnesota	161	72	89
Fordham	145	90	55
Southern California	142	60	82
Atlanta	137	130	7
Michigan	135	30	105
California	115	78	37
Boston University	111	55	56
Between 50 and 100 students			
Loyola (Chicago)	95	34	61
Simmons	90	85	5
Smith	89	89	0
Buffalo	81	21	60
National Catholic	81	67	14
Indiana	75	24	51
William and Mary	71	33	38
Denver	68	33	35
St. Louis	68	36	32
North Carolina	65	65	0
Toronto	65	55	10
Catholic University	60	28	32
Louisville	60	12	48
Louisiana	59	25	34
Ohio	55	46	9
Boston College	54	54	0
University of Washington	54	49	5
Fewer than 50 students			
Oklahoma	47	17	30
Nebraska	46	18	28
Bryn Mawr	45	24	21
Howard	38	13	25
Utah	35	9	26
Montreal	23	14	9
Carnegie	20	14	6

[a] Data from "Report on Students in Schools of Social Work, November 1, 1941,"
in News Letter, American Association of Schools of Social Work, December 1, 1941,
pp. 4–5.

Five schools had more than 200 students, and nine had between 100 and 200. In contrast with these 14 largest institutions, there were no fewer than 24 schools the enrollments of which did not exceed 100, and among them were seven schools with enrollments under 50. If consideration is limited to full-time students in these 38 schools, the picture looks even less bright. Only Chicago, New York, Western Reserve, Atlanta, and Pennsylvania, reported more than 100 such students, although Tulane would have moved into the category had it had two more matriculants. Fourteen schools had between 50 and 100 full-time students, and 19 schools had fewer than 50.

Examination of these figures immediately raises pertinent questions. Are student enrollments adequate in more than half the schools to permit the university to provide sound professional training or even to warrant its attempting to provide such training at all? In those schools that are primarily dependent on fees as a source of income, how many students are necessary to supply funds sufficient to maintain a competent faculty, not overburdened with hours of teaching and large enough to represent the several specialties of social work? In universities that are largely subsidized by tax funds, should the administration allocate considerable sums to struggling schools of social work or should the money go to other professional schools where the number of suitable applicants often exceeds the number that can be admitted with present facilities? These are questions with which the school and the university must struggle. It is obvious, however, that most of the small schools are now obliged to economize in teaching personnel and equipment to such a degree that their professional training suffers.

Why do enrollments remain so small in a period when social work is undergoing rapid expansion? Among the 26 schools that have maintained membership continuously in the national association from 1934 to 1941, there has been a slow, but unbroken, decrease rather than increase in enrollment. This trend is shown by the aggregate November figures in Table 5.

TABLE 5.—AGGREGATE NOVEMBER ENROLLMENT OF STUDENTS MAJORING IN SOCIAL WORK IN 26 IDENTICAL ASSOCIATION SCHOOLS, 1934 TO 1941

Year	Students majoring in social work
1934	5,091
1935	5,044
1936	4,732
1937	4,590
1938	4,462
1939	4,356
1940	4,312
1941	4,223

The year 1934, it is true, was not representative since enrollments were considerably swollen by students holding state and federal scholarships. Toward the end of the decade, furthermore, as schools shifted to a graduate basis of training, some temporary decrease in matriculation was to be expected. Even after consideration has been given to these factors, however, the enrollment trend of the last eight years has not been encouraging, particularly when it is noted that almost all of those schools which entered the Association subsequent to 1934, and all non-member schools, have been and still are small schools.

TABLE 6.—STUDENTS RECEIVING SPECIFIED RECOGNITION ON COMPLETION OF COURSES IN ASSOCIA-
TION SCHOOLS, ACADEMIC YEARS 1932–1933, 1935–1936, 1940–1941,[a] BY SCHOOLS

School	1932–1933				1935–1936				1940–1941			
	Ph.D.	M.A. or M.S.	Diploma or certificate	B.A. B.S. or Ph.B.	Ph.D.	M.A. or M.S.	Diploma or certificate	B.A. B.S. or Ph.B.	Ph.D.	M.A. or M.S.	Diploma or certificate	B.A. B.S. or Ph.B.
Type I schools												
Howard	—	—	—	—	—	—	—	—	—	—	5	—
Louisiana	—	—	—	—	—	—	—	—	—	6	—	—
Oklahoma	—	—	—	—	—	—	—	—	—	4	9	—
Utah	—	—	—	—	—	—	—	—	—	7	16	—
Type II schools												
Atlanta	—	—	21	—	—	—	22	—	—	19	14	—
Boston College	—	—	—	—	—	—	—	—	—	36	—	—
Boston Univ.	—	1	—	—	—	—	—	—	—	31	—	—
Bryn Mawr	—	—	4	—	—	—	7	—	—	4	10	—
Buffalo	—	—	—	—	—	—	11	12	—	10	38	—
California	—	—	29	—	1	1	52	—	—	2	69	—
Carnegie	—	—	—	7	—	—	—	8	—	7	—	12
Catholic Univ.	—	—	—	14	—	—	—	6	3	13	—	—
Chicago	2	19	—	—	1	56	—	—	2	119	—	4
Cincinnati	—	7	—	—	—	7	10	6	—	—	—	—
Denver	—	7	—	—	—	4	—	—	—	3	—	—
Fordham	1	1	10	5	—	18	27	—	—	24	18	—
Indiana	—	4	—	—	—	—	—	13	—	7	—	—
Jewish	—	—	15	—	—	5	7	—	—	—	—	—
Louisville	—	—	—	6	—	6	—	—	—	3	7	—
Loyola	—	2	—	—	—	2	—	12	—	8	—	—
Michigan	—	1	15	42	—	—	30	52	—	7	—	—
Minnesota	—	—	—	39	—	—	16	37	—	12	9	—

TABLE 6 (*Continued*)

School	1932–1933				1935–1936				1940–1941			
	Ph.D.	M.A. or M.S.	Diploma or certificate	B.A. B.S. or Ph.B.	Ph.D.	M.A. or M.S.	Diploma or certificate	B.A. B.S. or Ph.B.	Ph.D.	M.A. or M.S.	Diploma or certificate	B.A. B.S. or Ph.B.
Missouri	—	1	—	16	—	6	—	22	—	—	—	—
Montreal	—	—	—	—	—	—	—	—	—	—	11	—
National Catholic	—	9	3	—	—	8	5	—	—	27	9	—
Nebraska	—	—	—	—	—	—	—	—	—	2	9	—
New York	—	—	63	—	—	—	105	—	—	160	47	—
North Carolina	—	—	—	—	—	—	7	7	1	2	—	—
Northwestern	—	—	—	—	—	—	1	27	—	2	—	—
Ohio	—	7	—	23	—	22	—	60	—	19	—	43
Pennsylvania	—	—	71	—	—	46	4	—	—	44	3	—
Pittsburgh	—	—	—	—	—	3	—	—	—	93	—	—
St. Louis	—	—	—	—	—	5	—	—	—	7	—	—
Simmons	—	11	21	47	—	11	13	9	—	25	—	1
Smith	—	47	1	—	—	64	3	69	—	52	—	—
Southern Calif.	—	2	16	13	—	18	51	—	—	13	24	—
Toronto	—	—	—	—	—	—	—	—	—	—	40	—
Tulane	—	11	1	—	—	10	—	—	—	24	—	—
Washington Univ.	—	6	—	10	—	2	—	33	—	34	—	5
Washington, Univ. of	—	—	—	—	—	—	—	3	—	1	—	1
Western Reserve	—	35	9	16	—	49	6	—	—	74	—	—
William and Mary	—	13	7	—	—	9	33	19	—	5	—	—
Wisconsin	—	2	—	17	—	—	—	24	—	—	—	—
Total	3	186	286	255	2	352	409	413	6	904	329	66
Grand total	25 schools—730				32 schools—1,176				38 schools—1,305			

ᵃ Data from mimeographed annual statements of American Association of Schools of Social Work. When no figures appear for a school for one of the years, the school did not hold membership in the Association at that time. Table 1 notes the year when each school now belonging to the Association was established, and the year when it was admitted to membership.

In recognition conferred upon students who complete training, there has been appreciable improvement. Table 6 shows that 1,305 degrees or certificates were awarded by Association schools in 1940–1941, as contrasted with 730, by a smaller number of member schools, to be sure, in 1932–1933. As a result of action that put member schools largely on a graduate basis by 1939, the number of persons graduated with a bachelor's degree has decreased greatly. Conversely, those with a master's degree have increased rapidly. Much of the gain in masters' degrees results, however, from the fact that the formerly independent New York, Pennsylvania, and Atlanta schools gained university affiliation during the period, and hence made that recognition, rather than the certificate, available to a considerable proportion of their graduates. When one considers the need of social work agencies, and of the professional schools themselves, for persons at the administrative, teaching, and research levels who have had prolonged training, students obtaining the doctorate remain distressingly few.

If examination is made of recognition conferred by schools individually, the small number of graduates of most of them gives as discouraging a picture as the number of their students. In 1940–1941, for example, 22 of the 38 institutions conferred fewer than 30 degrees or certificates, nine conferred between 30 and 50, and only seven conferred more than 50. The seven schools were responsible for granting 52 per cent of all recognition conferred, and two of the seven—New York and Chicago—granted 25 per cent of it.

Several explanations can be given for both the small enrollment in many of the schools, and the small percentage of students who carry their training to completion. Salaries in the categories of social work for which the schools have trained, it must be repeated, have not been sufficiently large, and opportunities for advancement not sufficiently numerous to stimulate much professional training on a graduate level. Regardless of the salary scale, many public agencies have been hesitant to set academic and professional standards of employment that would necessitate study in a school of social work.

Some schools, moreover, are so financially poor and have so little prestige that they are unable to attract many students. Others are so remote from areas of field work that they cannot readily provide more than a handful of students with field-work training. Several compete for students with older or better established schools close at hand. Schools in these three categories probably need to reconsider their purpose and function, and attempt to decide whether their existence is justified or not. In some sections of the United States, on the other hand, it has been seen that there are vast areas with no school of social work sufficiently developed to meet the requirements for membership of the national association.

In our opinion some of the primary reasons why enrollments remain small in more than half the schools are: lack of effective methods for informing the public about social work and the need for professionally trained persons; failure of the schools to cultivate sufficiently vital contacts with their own universities and departments of social science; and inattention of the schools to recruiting of students from the undergraduate colleges. Social work is a new profession about which even college students know so little that many who are admirably fitted for it drift into other types of training. The university has not yet begun to draw public attention to its school of social work as it has to the medical, law, and engineering schools. Vocational counselors and faculty advisers in the social sciences have not been adequately encouraged to discuss with students the advisability of entering social work as a profession. Although more than 100 colleges and universities have assumed responsibility for offering a course that surveys the field of social work, the number is small when compared with the total number of institutions of higher learning in the United States. The American Association of Schools of Social Work, from which the several member schools might rightfully expect guidance in the recruitment of students, has been so busied with attempting to improve the schools themselves that it has up to the present time given little attention to the obtaining of students. Gratifying consideration of recruitment is now being undertaken by it.

NATIONAL ASSOCIATIONS

National associations in social work have been traditionally of two types. Those of the first type are primarily associations of agencies, and they are concerned with improving the professional quality of the work of their member agencies and with extending the scope of social work in their particular areas. Those of the second type are composed wholly or principally of individual social workers, whom they strive to assist in professional development, and in bettering conditions under which work is done. They also seek to improve and extend the social services.

The Family Welfare Association of America is an illustration of the first type. Some 200 local private and public family welfare agencies, as well as 700 lay and professional persons, hold membership in it.[1] In order to promote the development of family social work, the Association maintains a staff of field workers who aid local agencies throughout the United States and Canada; it assists in the development of qualified personnel in family case work; it provides an information service on family social work problems; it interprets to the public the family welfare movement; and it issues perhaps the most influential social work periodical, The Family, and other literature designed to help professional paid workers, volunteers, and lay persons serving on the executive boards of agencies practicing any form of social case work.

The number of national associations of this first type is difficult to determine, because a great many organizations, particularly in the fields of education-recreation and of health, interest themselves in varying degrees with social work. In his recent article entitled "National Associations in Social Work," David H. Holbrook concluded that there were about 50.[2] This conclusion was based, in large part, on a count of the associations which have membership in the National Social Work Council, National Health Council, and National Education-Recreation Council. Since the appearance of his article, a fourth council—the Social Case Work Council of National Agencies—has been formed to advance the competence of those national bodies primarily concerned with case work. In April, 1941, it had a constituency of 10, only four of which were not already members of one of the other councils.

[1] "Family Welfare Association of America," in Social Work Year Book, 1941, pp. 665–666.
[2] In Social Work Year Book, 1941, p. 365.

One association which, in our opinion, should be classified in the first group, regardless of the fact that it does not hold membership in any of the councils, is the American Association of Schools of Social Work. Its scope is nationwide, and its members are those professional schools which have proved themselves able to meet its established requirements for admission. Previous references have indicated how important is this organization in formulating standards of social work education. So vital to the future progress of social work practice is the body which concerns itself with professional training that space will be taken to discuss in detail its history and present program.

Under the second type of national association, four organizations should be included.[1] There is the American Association of Medical Social Workers, with some 1,700 active members, which provides means of communication among the personnel of this specialized field and which attempts to maintain and improve standards of social work in hospitals and dispensaries, and the medical social work which is now required in many public assistance agencies; the American Association of Psychiatric Social Workers, which performs a similar function for its 500 members; the American Association of Visiting Teachers whose 200 members are concerned with case work and caseworkers in the schools; and finally, the American Association of Social Workers, open to all social workers, regardless of the kind of work done or the agency represented, who can meet the requirements for membership.[2] The function and program

---

[1] Figures cited in this paragraph have been taken from the Directories of Agencies in Social Work Year Book, 1941.

[2] Another national organization which should be mentioned here is the American Association for the Study of Group Work, established in

of this last named body will also receive detailed subsequent attention.

In addition to these two clearly defined types of associations are trade unions in social work which gained a good deal of strength during the last decade. Although they differ from the traditional national associations to a considerable extent in purpose, in requirements for membership, and in techniques for promoting plans of action and influencing public opinion, they may, nevertheless, be considered as a third type of national organization—and one, the influence of which for social work cannot be disregarded. Hence, the evolution of the trade union movement in social work will be portrayed.

So will the work of the National Conference of Social Work. The Conference is scarcely more of an association in the customary sense than are trade unions in social work, although the national office is gradually assuming some of the broader functions which generally characterize associations. Its great contribution still lies in the annual meetings it holds. These have played so considerable a role in the fashioning of the profession of social work that something of its history is included in this section on nationwide organizations.

American Association of Schools of Social Work

In 1919 a group of independent schools or departments of colleges and universities, offering at least a minimum of preparation for social work, accepted an invitation to form

1936 and with a membership of more than 900 individual persons. It is a voluntary association of those interested in the study of the philosophy and practice of group work. Although its present function does not extend farther, it may develop into an association of group workers.

the Association of Training Schools of Professional Social Work. In 1933 the name of the organization was shortened to its present title. Some of the original members survived for only a short time. Of the 42 schools now belonging to the Association, 18 were organized by 1919, but only 11 have had continuous membership in the Association from that time. The one requirement for eligibility to membership set down in 1919 was that a school maintain a full-time course of training for social work which covered at least one academic year and included a substantial amount both of class instruction and of supervised field work.

For almost a decade the Association was little more than a conference of representatives of schools of social work, many of whom held widely divergent views concerning the nature and content of professional training. So strongly individualistic were the schools that it had been a distinct forward step when they exhibited a willingness to join an organization created to formulate group standards. Not until 1927, however, was the Association able to raise requirements for admission. And when these new requirements were finally promulgated, they were applicable only to new members and not to those admitted earlier than 1927. So little control did the Association exercise over its constituency that as late as 1934, several institutions belonged to it that would have been totally unable to meet the entrance requirements then in effect.

Recognition of the fact that control of member schools was almost non-existent had led in 1933 to the adoption of a plan for provisional membership. Accordingly, a school which has been approved by the Executive Committee and elected to membership by the Association is now admitted as a provisional member for a period of three years. It has, however, all the rights and privileges of full membership. At the end of three years its work is reviewed by the Executive Committee. If it is found satisfactory, the Committee then recommends the school for full membership at the next meeting of the Association.

A more significant step than creation of provisional membership was taken, in 1934, in what has proved to be the most successful attempt the national organization has yet made to elevate the standards of its constituency. By amendment of the by-laws, the Association gained authority to require its members to maintain the same standards as those demanded of schools applying for admission. Members that did not meet these standards were to have three years in which to modify their program. They might thereafter be dropped, either because of unsatisfactory standards or because of inactivity, provided that:

1. The Executive Committee study the situation of the school and present its findings to the Association with recommendations of action;

2. The school in question be notified that its case is to be considered, and be given a hearing before the Executive Committee if desired;

3. The school be given an extension of time, not to exceed one year from the date of notification of unsatisfactory standards, if in the judgment of the Executive Committee such extension be desirable and justified;

4. A school be dropped from membership at a regular meeting of the Association, and that such action shall require a vote of a majority of the member schools before becoming effective.[1]

[1] American Association of Schools of Professional Social Work: Constitution and By-Laws Adopted December 29, 1931, as Amended to January, 1942.

Admission requirements have been restudied and changes made upon several occasions since 1927. In order to gain membership under current regulations, a school must have been in existence for at least two academic years and be part of a college or university approved by the Association of American Universities. It must also meet the following requirements:

1. *Organization Requirements*

a. An organic grouping of relevant courses of instruction into a separate curriculum for the stated purpose of professional education for social work.

b. An administrator or director chosen or appointed as the executive head of the school, who is empowered, in co-operation with the faculty of the school, to exercise control over admission requirements to courses of instruction within the limits of university regulations. Criteria for determining qualifications for the Director shall include professional experience, graduate study, and familiarity with problems of education.

c. A suitable faculty which may be composed of full-time and part-time instructors, provided that at least two persons in Type I schools and three in Type II give their full time to the work of the school.

(1) Instruction in fundamental social work methods and the practice of social work shall be given by persons who have had valid and authoritative experience in social work.

(2) Instruction in other courses in the curriculum shall be given by persons equally qualified in their respective fields.

d. An annual budget for teaching and administrative salaries which can be shown to be adequate to carry out the program of the school.

e. The school shall furnish satisfactory assurance, in writing, of continued maintenance from a responsible college or university covering a period of not less than three years following the date of admission.

2. *Requirements for Admission of Students*

At least 90 per cent of the total number of students, enrolled in courses in the professional curriculum for which credit is given toward a degree or a certificate, shall have received a bachelor's degree or its academic equivalent in an approved college or university.

3. *Curriculum Requirements*

a. Type I schools must provide a curriculum covering not less than one academic year of graduate professional social work. Type II schools must provide not less than two years. In both types of school the requirements of the basic minimum curriculum must be met.

b. Field work

(1) Both types shall present an approved program of field work under the educational direction of the school.

(2) Field work shall be planned and supervised experience in the practice of social work as social work is carried on currently by recognized social agencies.[1]

By making small changes in or additions to the by-laws as frequently as the majority of the membership deem such changes desirable, the Association has succeeded in creating standards that conform in general outline to those of other types of professional education. Some of the specific standards, however, are still very low and must be raised whenever conditions permit. Two full-time faculty members for a Type I school and three for a Type II school are unquestionably not enough for any institution seriously engaged in providing professional education. The earlier requirement that a school have an annual budget amounting to at least $10,000 has been altered to ability to show that the budget is adequate for carrying out the educational program. Unfortunately schools are still accepted for membership when

[1] *Ibid.*

available funds are too small for such administrative, teaching, research, and clerical personnel as are generally deemed essential for maintenance of substantial professional training.

Mention has been made in earlier pages of the Association's long and courageous attempt to raise social work training from an undergraduate to a graduate level. Concerning the desirability of such an attempt there is little question and much warm commendation. The concentrated effort generally required to elevate standards, however, sometimes results in focusing attention so exclusively upon the task that realistic appraisal of the needs of various parts of the country is lost from sight. No better illustration could be given than that of control of medical education. As a result of Abraham Flexner's portrayal in 1910 of distressing conditions in many medical schools and subsequent action by the Council on Medical Education and Hospitals of the American Medical Association, schools, poor educationally or financially, were forced to close their doors with amazing rapidity. Between 1910 and 1930 the number decreased from 131 to 76. Only those institutions that could meet high and progressively higher standards received or continue to receive the Council's approval. To be listed annually by the Council assures a school of great prestige and the public of excellence of education. But the action taken was so drastic that many regions were left without needed training facilities, while fees and requirements for admission became so high in the remaining schools that many prospective physicians were excluded. This situation probably encouraged the founding of new types of schools—the schools of the "healing cults"—over which the Council has no control and of the soundness of which society has little guarantee. Thus, one of the most sincere and successful attempts ever made to raise standards of professional education appears in retrospect to have accomplished the wiping out of too many useful, though admittedly inferior, institutions, and to have provided opportunity for the creation of even less desirable forms of training.

Organizations concerned with progress in professional education have a dual responsibility to society: responsibility for the improvement as well as the maintenance of standards in the more favored institutions, and also for the upbuilding of training in those areas where professional development is backward. By making social work education on a graduate level an entirely rigid prerequisite for admission to membership, the American Association of Schools of Social Work may unconsciously be doing the profession of social work a disservice. Latent in the philosophy that actuated the Association to create two types of membership lies the possibility for further extension of types. Establishment of a third category would provide opportunity for membership to those schools, already discussed, that are earnestly striving to promote social work training in regions where standards of practice and salaries do not yet warrant much, if any, graduate education.

The Association has never made provision for admission of schools that specialize exclusively in group work. Because case work has always been considered, within the Association, the keystone on which rests professional training in social work, group-work schools have remained outside the traditional pattern. The fact that such schools frequently train persons for positions in group education and recreation as well as in social work has also complicated the problem. In recent years, however, certain developments have occurred that cannot be overlooked. The demand for group workers has increased rapidly. Thus existing schools, like George Williams College, have been able to attract larger numbers of students and to strengthen their curriculum; new training facilities, such as those at Temple University, have appeared; several of the Association schools of social work have introduced extensive offerings in group work.

In the meantime, a generic concept of group work has emerged. Agencies employing the group-work process have discovered that despite traditional differences, they share a common function. Certain basic assumptions, purposes, methods, techniques, and criteria are coming to be identified.[1] Group-work schools, as well as group-work agencies, are assuming responsibility for development of this generic concept and for training students in its understanding and utilization. Enough progress has been achieved in professionalizing group work to make some of these specialized schools believe that they should be accorded membership in the Association. If not accorded membership, they are likely to create an association of their own. The question of eligibility to general membership or to membership in a further category, created expressly for the purpose, would seem to warrant the careful consideration of the national organization.

Since 1938 the Association has been able greatly to enlarge its work through employment of an executive secretary. As a result, member schools have been surveyed, advice

[1] Hendry, Charles E., "Social Group Work," in Social Work Year Book, 1941, p. 524.

and assistance have been given to schools desirous of becoming members, a large number of committees have more actively participated in the program of the Association, and the comprehensive research study, Education for the Public Social Services, has been brought to conclusion. In the field work and counseling that have been done, some persons see the beginning of a task that should assume much larger proportions in the future. They believe that the Association should embark upon systematic planning for the distribution of training facilities, as well as for the content of professional education. Such planning would be concerned with prevention of wasteful duplication of facilities, and also with the building of strong regional schools in undeveloped areas.

The geographical distribution of schools of social work is a matter of no small concern. Some sections are rich in opportunities for professional education, while others are poor. The northeast quarter of the United States has no fewer than 19 of the present 42 member schools. The three states of Massachusetts, New York, and Pennsylvania alone have 11 of the 19. In this same section, a number of additional colleges and universities are already giving some training in social work. A substantial survey of the current and prospective demand for social workers in the areas served by these schools, and also of the maximum training resources of existing institutions would seem to be urgently needed. On the basis of such a survey, the Association could more authoritatively acquaint colleges and universities, through counseling and printed literature, with the need for fewer, or more, training centers as the case might be. Many a college might be persuaded to set aside, for graduate scholarships in an approved existing school, money that would otherwise be spent in the administration of a meager social work curriculum.

In the other three quarters of the United States where schools are sparse, it is believed that the Association should encourage the creation of centrally located regional schools. Successful co-ordination of the educational facilities of two or more colleges, effected in recent years in various places, affords a helpful pattern which will probably be followed more frequently as a result of present economic exigencies. Particularly heartening is the plan for the new school of social work in Nashville, already mentioned, which is to be operated by the three neighboring institutions of higher learning.

It is not impossible, therefore, that the Association could influence regional groups of colleges and universities to operate schools jointly, or to designate particular schools as official training centers to which students would be sent on a scholarship basis. Several curricula already exist which might form the nuclei for accelerated growth. Their administrators have expressed the desire for sympathetic examination and aid. As in the case of the northeastern section, however, adequate surveys of existing conditions and needs are prerequisite to sound counseling and guidance, and solicitation of the active interest of state departments of public welfare in plans for any such regional schools would be highly desirable.

The most ambitious undertaking by the Association in curriculum planning is its recently completed study, Education for the Public Social Services.[1] Coincident with the

[1] University of North Carolina Press, Chapel Hill, 1942.

vast growth of public social work, we have seen that professional schools made varying degrees of effort to adapt their curricula to the new needs. However, social work practitioners, administrators of the public services recruited from other forms of training, and educators began to question the assumption that preparation for social work was the best training for the public services. Hence, the Association obtained a grant in 1938 from the Rockefeller Foundation for the purpose of studying the present and future role of schools of social work in educating personnel for such agencies.

Under the sponsorship of the Association, a Study Committee was appointed to assume general direction of the investigation. An advisory committee of 25 persons was also created, drawn from official and voluntary health, public welfare, public administration, and educational agencies; from professional associations in nursing, education, home economics, and statistics; and from the American Association of Social Workers. The research staff consisted of Marion Hathway, then executive secretary of the Association; Dorothy C. Kahn, then associate executive secretary of the American Association of Social Workers; and George C. S. Benson, then director of the Curriculum in Public Administration at the University of Michigan. Professor Hathway examined the training resources of the schools and prepared the final report; Miss Kahn and Professor Benson were largely responsible for examination of the personnel requirements of the public services.

The public services studied were limited primarily to those included under the Social Security Act. Public assistance and child welfare were found to have been greatly influenced by traditions of social work practice; unemployment compensation and employment service, and old-age insurance had been unaffected by methods of social work. As foregoing pages have indicated, the Study Committee concluded that the schools of social work could profitably prepare students for public and child welfare positions, with some assurance that such agencies would demand the services of trained social workers. Regarding preparation for the insurance and employment services, the Committee registered the fact that the schools were doing relatively little. Its report was not fertile in suggestions for methods of achieving greater rapport between these latter services and the schools, or in specific plans for training.

The study, which was made available to the writer in manuscript, has certain distinct shortcomings. As it suggests, examination of a greater number of the public social services would have been desirable. Memoranda of two or three pages only were devoted to the relation to social work of each of the following federal agencies: Bureau of Prisons, Federal Supervisor of Probation, Veterans' Administration, Vocational Rehabilitation of Disabled Persons, Office of Indian Affairs, Work Projects Administration, National Youth Administration, Farm Security Administration, and United States Housing Authority. State and local public welfare agencies whose functions have not grown out of the Social Security Act received no attention. The topic of treatment of juvenile delinquents and adult offenders was accorded one paragraph; social services in the public schools, and public health and medical services were reviewed in a little more detail. Administration of workmen's compensation, the oldest form of social insurance in the United

States, was illustrated by reference to procedure and personnel in New York State.[1]

Because of the imposed limitation of scope, even within the public services selected for study, the work of specialists was omitted. Hence social research positions were not examined. Neither was there examination of the medical social work provided by the Children's Bureau in its child welfare, and maternal and child health services, and in its program for crippled children.[2]

More important than the Association's failure to examine in detail a larger number of public social services was its omission of a comparative survey and an evaluation of effectiveness of other forms of training for public service, including curricula in public administration. Hence the Association was without supplementary criteria and points of view against which to measure its own assumptions and the degree of success of its schools. And the public was still left with the unanswered question of whether or not social work education is the best training for the great majority of the non-clerical positions in the expanding public welfare services.

Like many undertakings subject to group approval, the resolution of intellectual conflicts among members of the Study Committee resulted in extreme cautiousness and generalization of statement, when incisiveness would, perhaps, have been more helpful. The report points to alterations that need to be made within the existing curriculum, but it presents no model sketched in bold and imaginative design. Instead, it recommends that several further studies be undertaken.

[1] Education for the Public Social Services, pp. 246–280.
[2] Ibid., p. 30.

In spite of such shortcomings, the marked value of the report should not be minimized. The knowledge obtained of current training for social work, the counsel afforded many a school, the group effort resulting in a document to which the several members of the Committee were willing to subscribe—these are gains, the significance of which is apparent upon recalling the Association's ineptitude of only a decade and a half ago. Field surveys of the public services, creation of closer contacts between faculty members and administrators, and effort to envisage the nature and degree of responsibility of schools for the training of personnel represent accomplishments of considerable magnitude.

From the surveys have come numerous suggestions for reorientation of the curriculum. Reference has been made earlier in this study to the recommendation that public welfare should be a basic course required of all students; that preparation for rural social work be the subject of special inquiry; that the minimum curriculum be restudied. The Committee stated further that "areas in the curriculum related to special needs in the public social services require exploration and development. Among these are labor economics, medical economics, vocational guidance and aptitudes, occupational classification, industrial processes, procedural analysis in administration and finance."[1] Were the schools generally to accept but a few of these suggestions, the curriculum would bear a greatly altered appearance.

American Association of Social Workers

The American Association of Social Workers, with its approximately 90 chapters, is a second outstanding national

[1] *Ibid.,* p. 18.

organization concerned with raising the professional standards of social workers. The section of its constitution relating to its purposes, rewritten in 1939, reads as follows:

This corporation is an association of social workers meeting qualifications of training and experience, working in the area of human relationships, interested in advancing the quality of social service by means of individual and collective action in defining, promoting and protecting social work concepts and principles in the following areas: social work practice and the advancing body of knowledge and skills required in practice; personnel standards, including professional education; standards of organization and administration affecting practice; and social problems observed in social work practice.

The constitution states that membership shall be open to men and women trained in social work who are or have been professionally concerned with problems of social organization and adjustment.[1] The qualifications for membership, as defined in 1922, required that the applicant "must have had four years of practical experience in social organizations of recognized standing and have demonstrated that he possesses an educational background warranting expectation of success and progress in the profession of social work." Academic work and professional training could be substituted in part for the requirement of four years of practical experience. In no case, however, could an applicant be admitted who had had less than one year of social work experience.

The framers of the original constitution were faced with a problem that inevitably causes much difficulty for any nascent profession. What standards should social workers

[1] American Association of Social Workers, Constitution Adopted June 28, 1922.

choose as prerequisites for admission to their national organization which would not be too exclusive and which would, nevertheless, serve to raise the level of professional efficiency? The membership requirements that they set down and that remained valid until 1933 were extremely general. A judicious evaluation of applications for admission was a difficult task for the Membership Committee. The best that could be obtained under the constitution promulgated in 1922 was the exercise of a small degree of selection. Many considered that the acceptance of applicants on the basis of experience alone was unfortunate, since it opened the doors to large numbers of social workers who had had only apprenticeship training at the most, and who could not be considered professional in anything like the sense in which the term is used by older and more stable groups. It must be said, however, in extenuation of the attitude then taken, that the Association recognized the value of academic and professional training by making such education a partial substitute for practical experience. It was necessary that the emphasis should have been placed on experience rather than on training in a decade when schools were still inadequate and relatively few social workers had had any formal professional education.

After several years of deliberation the Association concluded that the time had come when its requirements for admission must be raised, and in 1929, the constitution was amended. According to the changes enacted in that year applicants for junior membership, after March 1, 1930, were to have the following qualifications:

1. Minimum age of twenty-one years.

2. Completion of at least two years' work in an approved college.

3. Three additional years of general education, technical training or employment in an approved agency. This requirement might be satisfied in either one of the two following ways:

a. Completion of two additional years' work in an approved college plus one year's work in an approved school of social work.

b. Three years spent in some combination of: attendance at an approved college, attendance at an approved school of social work, or employment in an approved agency, provided, however, that the applicant had satisfactorily completed:

> Fifteen semester hours of social and biological science in an approved school of social work or college;
>
> Ten semester hours of approved technical social work courses;
>
> Three hundred hours of supervised field work in connection with technical social work courses.

4. Employment at the time of application in an approved agency.

The changes in qualifications for full membership did not go into effect until July 1, 1933. Applicants after that date were required to meet the following requisites:

1. Completion of at least two years' work in an approved college.

2. Five additional years of general education, technical training or employment in an approved agency, or four additional years, if both college graduation and two years of graduate social work training were included.

The requirement of seven years might be satisfied in one of two ways:

a. Graduation from an approved college, plus one year in an approved school of social work, plus two years of employment in an approved agency.

b. Two years' work in an approved college, plus five years spent in some combination of: additional work in an approved college, attendance at an approved school of social work, or employment in an approved agency, provided, however, that the applicant had satisfactorily completed:

> Twenty semester hours of social and biological science in an approved college or school of social work.
>
> Twenty-four hours of approved technical social work courses.
>
> Three hundred hours of supervised field work in connection with technical social work courses.
>
> Two years of employment in an approved agency.

These requirements represent a real advance over those of 1922, but there are still many questions which await further consideration. The provision for junior membership was long criticized on the ground that agencies frequently were willing to substitute partial qualifications for membership, instead of full professional ones, as standards which applicants must meet in obtaining positions. When the proposal to discontinue junior membership was brought before the Delegate Conference in 1935, however, the majority was overwhelmingly opposed to it. Less has been heard about this issue in recent years. Since no one may maintain junior membership after becoming eligible for full membership or for a period of more than five years, considerable check is placed upon the relative number of such members. In October, 1941, they constituted only about 7 per cent of the total membership.

Academic work of a graduate nature other than in schools of social work is ignored in the requirements for membership, while graduation from a school of social work is not yet required. One of the encouraging aspects of the amendment to the constitution is the recognition of the importance of the social and biological sciences. This recognition is particularly valuable for the very reason that the professional schools have been lax regarding them. The Association has done nothing more, however, than to require a certain number of semester hours in any one or all of seven fields. The wisdom of a requirement stated in this way is questionable. There is generally small value in courses taken at random. Many an applicant will be easily able to furnish proof that he has had 20 semester hours of these sciences, but the knowledge of organic life, human behavior, or the social order which he may have gained from one course in zoology, and one or two in several of the social sciences is likely to be exceedingly vague.

Again, although the requirement of 20 semester hours of social and biological science is made of all who do not hold an academic degree, it is not a requirement for those who have been graduated from an approved college and from a two-year graduate school of social work. It cannot safely be taken for granted that even those in possession of a bachelor's degree and a professional certificate have had adequate work in these sciences. Although most universities have worked out well-differentiated curricula, it is quite possible to fill an undergraduate schedule with languages, literature, history, fine arts, and physical sciences to the neglect of the social and biological sciences. James E. Hagerty's study of the women graduates of 1928 and 1929 of six Ohio colleges and universities revealed that only one in ten had had any work in psychology, and only one in four in sociology. More than one-half of these women were without training in biology, nearly two-thirds were without any training in political science, and nearly three-fourths had not studied economics.[1]

"Three hundred hours of supervised field work in connection with technical social work courses" has been a condition effectively limiting membership in the Association, and the source of more problems than any other phrase in the present requirements. Under its first interpretation the Association accepted only field work done for credit under the supervision of an approved school of social work. This kept so many persons, who could meet the other qualifications, from becoming members that the national body decided to construe the definition a little more broadly to include supervised training not obtained as part of a school course, provided it had been acquired in an agency used by a professional school for field work. The Association required a statement from the agency to the effect that the applicant had received a degree of supervision comparable to that given to students in schools of social work.

Although this more flexible interpretation permitted a substantial number of persons to become junior members, it did not provide for regularly employed persons who had acquired the requisite amount of class work, generally as part-time students, but had not been able to obtain field work under supervision of a school or training in an agency used by a school. Consequently, in September, 1935, the national organization decided that for an experimental period it would accept what it termed "supervised practice" as fulfilling the requirement concerning field work. A person wishing to qualify for membership under this interpreta-

[1] Training of Social Workers. McGraw-Hill Book Co., New York, 1931, pp. 75–76.

tion was to notify the Association that he had been permitted by the agency employing him to spend six months of intensive work on a relatively small number of cases, and that provision had been made for weekly conferences with his supervisor.[1] This plan was not widely used because of the difficulty of meeting all the conditions and therefore it was discontinued three years later.

The problem of requirements for membership has been aggravated by the rapid expansion, since 1933, of public assistance, and to a lesser degree of social group work, probation and parole, and community organization. So unprecedented has been the growth of the public social services in the last decade that the majority of persons employed in them are unable to meet the qualifications for membership. Similarly, in group work and community organization many persons occupy responsible positions who cannot obtain membership because of their lack of professional training in an approved school of social work. Some of these persons have completed the course of study in schools devoted exclusively to group-work education. But since these schools have never been officially recognized by either the American Association of Schools of Social Work or the American Association of Social Workers, their graduates are not eligible for membership.

An educational and occupational analysis made by the Association of the 791 new members admitted in 1940 revealed that 348 were employed in public social work, 412 represented private agencies, and the remaining 31 were

---

[1] "300 Hours of Supervised Field Work," in The Compass, May, 1935, pp. 7–8.

students or not at the time employed.[1] Only 24 representatives of group work and 14 of community organization were included. Although the figure for public social workers was less than that for private workers, it can be considered small only in relation to the total number of persons engaged in public welfare who were ineligible for membership. Those in group work and community organization who achieved membership were actually and relatively few. It is essential to note, however, that prior to 1933, when admission was on the basis of experience rather than of professional preparation, the organization did not succeed in enlisting support from any considerable number of representatives of these two fields.

In recent years there has been a perhaps small but insistent demand that the national body accord greater recognition to the newer fields of social work, and some concerted pressure has been exercised to gain such recognition. Because of the fact that social work has developed more rapidly and in rather different directions than had been foreseen, the Association has found itself with inadequately developed policies concerning its responsibility to those persons who do not meet the specific requirements already formulated. Hence, it has been caught in the dilemma of being asked somewhat emphatically to decide whether its particular educational standards should be maintained in the face of excluding so many persons occupying social work positions, or whether the basis of membership should be "broadened" to include persons with diverse backgrounds in education and experience.

[1] "Qualifications of 791 New Members Admitted During 1940," in The Compass, February–March, 1941, p. 22.

No definitive answer has been given. At the Delegate Conference of 1940, however, the Association adopted a statement of purpose and membership policy designed to clarify its position.[1] This statement reaffirmed the conviction of the Association that it "should continue as a general professional organization requiring a selected membership standard," deemed essential for the realization of its purposes and for reliable service to social work clients and the general public. The document recognized the fact that many persons of ability and experience were excluded under the present requirements, but noted that any method of selective admission would exclude some such persons. It spoke of the various organizations seeking a comprehensive membership through which they might contribute to the progress of social work. The statement concluded with the assertion that "selection should be based on the objective of increasingly greater adequacy and responsibility in social workers"; that such selection should seek to secure a membership "whose program and activities will be founded on basic concepts of social work as they develop in all fields" and which will "recognize the relation between these basic concepts and a common educational foundation."

The foregoing discussion indicates that much still remains to be done if the American Association of Social Workers is to succeed in building up a membership of well-qualified persons drawn from all the various fields. But one should not think that the advances achieved thus far have been won without much effort. In spite of the fact that the organization has been crippled by a lack of financial re-

---

[1] "Purpose and Membership Selection," in The Compass, June–July, 1940, p. 12.

sources, it has made a valiant attempt to raise standards. Its program, however, has frequently met with unfavorable criticism. There was fear at the beginning of the decade that the enforcement of higher entrance requirements would reduce the number of applicants in too drastic a manner. There was the demand, already noted, at the close of the decade, that admission requirements be reformulated to permit broader eligibility. The fear of the early 1930's has not been realized. A membership of 5,000 in 1930 had grown to 11,035 in October, 1941.

Note should be made parenthetically of the distribution of these 11,035 members, since this distribution offers substantial evidence about the areas where professional social work has made its greatest advances.[1] Slightly more than half of the total membership of October, 1941, was in the six states of New York, Illinois, Pennsylvania, California, Ohio, and Missouri. These are large states having one or more great metropolitan cities, and they are in general highly industrialized. Hence it is not surprising that each of them had more than 500 social workers who held membership in the Association, while New York had 1,650. How many additional workers were eligible for membership is not known. Nineteen states had between 100 and 500 members. These two groups of states accounted for 81 per cent of the entire membership. Scarcely more than 2,000 members were located in the remaining 24 states, the territorial possessions of the United States, and Canada. Fifteen small, sparsely settled, or largely agricultural states had fewer than 50 members each.

[1] Statistics of membership by states, as of October 22, 1941, furnished by the Association.

Members of the Association are also members of state, local, or territorial chapters, except in a few places where national membership is still too sparse to warrant creation of chapters. In its early years the activities of the Association tended to center in the national office in New York, but gradually increased participation of chapters has evolved. They are now recognized as the basic units through which the program of the Association is carried on. Because of radical variations in size and structure and in financial and professional resources, the degree of participation differs widely among them. Much remains to be done in aiding them to make full use of their potentialities.[1] A forward step was taken in 1934 when plans were perfected for an annual Delegate Conference, composed of representatives from chapters and from non-chapter areas in proportion to number of members. The conference now serves as the official means through which the membership acts on all matters of national policy and program.

The program of the Association is devoted to the professional development of social workers and to the promotion of more adequate social services.[2] To achieve these purposes the national body engages in such research, publication, and field work as its budget permits. Emphasis is placed upon interpretation of the function, qualifications and status of practicing social workers, and upon questions of public policy which relate to the social services. The Association has published a series of analytical studies of positions, popu-

---

[1] Johnson, Glenna B., "Report for the Committee on Chapters," in The Compass, August, 1941, pp. 14–18.
[2] For a more detailed statement than appears in these pages, see Arlien Johnson's "Social Work as a Profession," in Social Work Year Book, 1941, pp. 548–551.

larly spoken of as job analyses, in the major fields of social work. It has made extensive surveys of need for and administration of relief in various parts of the United States, and the proceedings of the Delegate Conference of 1936 were published under the title, This Business of Relief. The Compass, the monthly bulletin sent to all members, contains some material of current interest on social work topics in general, as well as news of the business of the Association, and of projects that the organization is furthering through committees and local chapters.

In recent years much of the work of the Association has fallen within the three program divisions that have been created: Employment Practices, Personnel Standards, and Government and Social Work. Since employment practices determine to no small degree the type of person attracted to an agency and his ability to work competently and to develop professionally, the Association has always been concerned with the definition and promotion of sound practices.[1] In 1937 it made formal declaration of principles designed as a guide to acceptable standards. Three years later the Delegate Conference resolved that:

A social agency should have a written statement of formulated employment policies which embodies the current operating practices of the agency. . . . This statement should be available to all the staff of the agency and to applicants for employment and should constitute a part of the employment agreement, whether verbal or written, which defines the obligations accepted by the employer and employee at the time of employment.[2]

[1] See Walter M. West's paper, Responsibility of the AASW for Standards of Employment Practices, read before the Boston Chapter, December 17, 1940. Copies may be obtained from the AASW office.

[2] "Agency Standards for Employment Conditions." Reprinted from The Compass, June–July, 1940.

The work of the Association in reference to personnel standards has included study of personnel needs, consultation regarding and formulation of standards for civil service and merit systems, interpretation of the value of qualified personnel, and close co-operation with the American Association of Schools of Social Work in analyzing basic concepts of theory and practice. In 1940 the Delegate Conference issued a statement on standards for social work personnel that defined the professional preparation or experience which should be sought by an agency in filling social work positions. It noted, furthermore, that standards for selection of personnel should be considered as evolutionary, and hence subject to continuous review. It also asserted that "requirements of state and local residence, veterans preference and other extra-professional considerations are inimical to selection of personnel on the basis of professional competence."[1]

Through the division of Government and Social Work, established in 1934, the Association has interested itself in efforts to improve the economic conditions of the unemployed and to provide greater social security for groups most subject to misfortune. These efforts indicate that the organization has committed itself to use its power and influence for the solution of economic and social problems as well as to raise professional standards. The entire program of the Delegate Conference of 1936 was devoted to a survey of the situation concerning relief among the unemployed and to the formulation of plans for re-establishing relief on a national basis. The press, radio, and other re-

[1] "AASW Statement on Standards for Social Work Personnel." Reprinted from The Compass, June–July, 1940.

sources were utilized for setting forth the conviction of delegates that there must be a system of federal grants-in-aid to
states for public assistance of the needy, and that these
grants should not be a substitute for federal employment,
but a further means of providing a well-rounded program of
social security. The action of this conference, like earlier activity by the Association which materially influenced federal
and state relief policy during the depression years, emphasizes how far the organization has gone in concerning itself
with great national issues.

In recent years the division of Government and Social
Work has been charged with responsibility for formulating
a Platform on Public Social Services. This Platform is presented annually to the Delegate Conference for discussion,
revision, and approval. Hence, it may be considered a
résumé of the principles of the Association in reference to
such services. A summary of the Platform, as amended in
1941, follows:[1]

All persons, regardless of race, creed, or any other condition,
who are unable to secure suitable employment or whose resources fall below a level sufficient to maintain them and their
families in health, decency and socially acceptable activity are a
proper charge upon public resources. Work should be available
to all who are not disabled. To the extent that private industry
cannot provide work, government should furnish it.

Provisions for insurance against loss of income because of unemployment, old age, industrial injury, and death or disablement
of breadwinner should be extended to cover disability and illness; should be adequate in amount and period of time to provide reasonable security for the insured; and should apply to the

[1] "AASW Position on Public Social Services," in The Compass, August, 1941, pp. 25–27.

entire working population. Public assistance should be available —regardless of cause of need, race, creed, political affiliation, citizenship, length and place of residence, or other arbitrary restriction on eligibility—to meet the needs of all those unable in other ways to maintain for themselves and their dependents an adequate standard of living.

Employment service under public auspices and on a nation-wide basis is essential for the guidance and distribution of the labor supply in relation to the requirements of the labor market. Adequate employment data and current inventories of occupational shortages are necessary for the promotion of effective employment service.

Government should make available safe, decent low-rent housing, and medical and public health services to those not otherwise provided with adequate shelter and health care. It should, furthermore, provide facilities and leadership for public recreation as one of the basic requirements of a well-rounded public welfare program.

In order to carry out the foregoing program, a co-ordinated administrative structure is essential in federal, state, and local units of government. Federal resources, administrative and financial, should be drawn upon to equalize the resources of state and local governments, to help establish minimum standards of operation and service, and to provide a central agency for necessary research and planning.

The public interest demands competent personnel in order that funds for the social services may be administered humanely, economically, and effectively. Professional functions should be performed by professionally qualified persons. A well-administered merit system offers the only assurance of such personnel in the public service.

NATIONAL CONFERENCE OF SOCIAL WORK

The National Conference of Charities and Correction, the name of which in 1917 became the National Conference of Social Work, was founded nearly seven decades ago. An informal meeting of the State Boards of Charities of Wisconsin, Illinois, and Michigan had been called in the spring of 1872 for a mutual exchange of ideas concerning their work and programs. The experience was so profitable that a second meeting was held the following spring. This led, in turn, to the First National Conference of Charities, which convened in New York City in 1874 in connection with the meeting of the American Social Science Association. Nineteen persons were present representing four states. Previous to 1879, at which date the Conference became an independent body, it had been composed of representatives of state boards of charities, heads of state institutions, and members of the American Social Science Association. Thereafter, delegates began to be appointed by governors of jurisdictions that had no state boards of charities. The relationship between the Conference and these boards for many years was very close and the Conference was indirectly responsible for the creation of a number of such boards. Conference programs were of particular interest to their representatives and to institutional executives. At nearly every annual convention, there were addresses on the functions of state boards of charities, on the care of the mentally ill, care of dependent and delinquent children, prison reform, crime, pauperism, immigration, and so on.

As the years advanced and social work became more diversified, the problems of state institutions, institutional care, and legislative reform gradually received relatively less attention at the annual meetings. In the Conference of 1880 there was, for the first time, a committee that was concerned with the organization of charities in cities where they did not

exist. Thereafter, this subject was a definite part of the discussion of each annual program. It not only created tremen-
dous interest, but it stimulated immeasurably the establishing of charity organization societies from city to city.[1]

In 1917, when the Conference was altered in name to that
which it now bears, it was organized in permanent divisions
or sections representing various fields of social work. The
following list of the divisions of the Conference of 1934
gives some indication of the topics on which social work had
come to concentrate attention:[2]

Children
Delinquents and Correction
Health
The Family
Industrial and Economic Prob-
lems
Neighborhood and Commu-
nity Life
Educational Publicity

Mental Hygiene
Organization of Social Forces
Administration of Public So-
cial Work
The Immigrant
The American Indian
Professional Standards and
Education

The Conference held in Montreal in 1935 initiated a
radical departure from past practices in the arrangement of
its program. In order to integrate this program by stressing
only the major fields of social work, it abolished the customary divisions. In their place it substituted four broad sections: Social Case Work, Social Group Work, Community
Organization, and Social Action. Under these heads all ad-

[1] Hart, Hastings H., "President's Address: The Relation of the National Conference of Charities and Correction to the Progress of the
Past Twenty Years," in Proceedings of the National Conference of Charities and Correction, 1893, pp. 1–28.
[2] "National Conference of Social Work," in The Conference Bulletin, April, 1934, sec. 2, pp. 16–18.

dresses and discussions were grouped. A fifth section, Public Welfare Administration, was added a year later. Since then the sections have remained unchanged, but their programs are customarily supplemented by others designed by special committees whose work is considered of significant interest at the time. Thus, in 1942, open meetings were sponsored by committees on the Alien and Foreign-Born Citizen, Children's Institutions, Conservation of Family Finances and Resources, Interstate Migration, Law and Social Work, the Physically Handicapped, Prevention and Treatment of Delinquency and Crime.

The Proceedings of the National Conference are published annually, and include papers selected from those read at the preceding convention. A quarterly bulletin is also issued as a house organ.

During recent years the Conference, through its office in Columbus, Ohio, has extended service to state conferences of social work. Bulletins discussing problems faced by state conference secretaries are distributed, a handbook to aid those responsible for conducting conferences has been published, a clearing house for exchange of material among secretaries is maintained, and regional meetings for executives are held annually in the hope of thus improving state conferences.[1]

An evaluation of the influence which the National Conference has had upon American social work is almost an impossibility. It is not so much a national organization as a public forum, which "exists to facilitate discussion of the problems and methods of practical human improvement, to

[1] Close, Kathryn, "Conferences of Social Work," in Social Work Year Book, 1941, p. 135.

increase the efficiency of agencies and institutions devoted to this cause, and to disseminate information."[1] The very fact that it is a forum, and that it takes no action on public or legislative questions by resolution or otherwise, renders its influence elusive. So many of its results have been indirect or intangible that there is no way of measuring them. Reports have been received time and again, however, of the effect which some paper read at the Conference has had in changing legislation or in shaping policies and plans. One of the most clearly defined indications of its success is the large attendance at its annual meeting, which is held in an important city of the United States or Canada. No convention is likely to survive for nearly seventy years and grow in attendance from 19 to several thousand—the largest registered attendance was 6,670 in 1936—unless its program has deeply significant and vital merit. Its present membership, both of individuals and of organizations, represents nearly every state in the United States, Cuba, Hawaii, the Philippines, Canada, and other countries.

In 1893 when Hastings H. Hart reviewed the history of the first twenty years of the Conference, he attributed its success to certain distinctive characteristics, which most of its present members would probably agree still distinguish it. He spoke of its catholicity, which permitted the expression of attitudes and philosophies by widely divergent religious, political, and social welfare groups. Its optimism served as a lever to raise its constituency above the discouraging aspects of their daily routine and to give them encouragement for the furtherance of the social good. Its practicality resulted in a realistic rather than a visionary consid-

[1] National Conference of Social Work, Constitution and By-Laws.

eration of the problems before it, and this realism tended to be subsequently translated into constructive action. Its personnel was largely drawn from men and women of ability, experience, and broad perspective. Finally, its simplicity of organization freed it from time-consuming parliamentary wrangles and long business meetings.[1]

Trade Unions in Social Work

Late in 1930 there was launched in New York City a Social Workers' Discussion Club as "an open forum for the analysis of basic social problems and their relation to social work." This was the beginning of a rapid growth of organizations composed of rank-and-file social workers and other employes of social work agencies. By April, 1936, the movement had gained such momentum that Social Work Today, then its official organ,[2] reported the existence of 43 groups in 22 cities, six groups in counties, and three representing the entire country. The total membership was thought to be about 15,000. Although these groups were known by a multiplicity of names and their purposes differed to a considerable degree, the majority were protective organizations. Most of their members were employes of public relief agencies. Several of the groups that began as forums for discussion had become occupied with protective functions; others that were formed in the interest of better salaries, improved working conditions, and "job security" had assumed educational functions. As a whole, they were concerned by 1936

[1] Hart, Hastings H., "President's Address: The Relation of the National Conference of Charities and Correction to the Progress of the Past Twenty Years," in Proceedings of the National Conference of Charities and Correction, 1893, pp. 28–31.
[2] A monthly publication begun in March, 1934.

both with questions of their own occupational status and with more adequate provisions for general social welfare.[1]

The basic unity underlying the objectives of these groups early suggested the desirability of some form of national organization. Consequently, in February, 1935, delegates from 30 rank-and-file associations met in Pittsburgh for their first national convention. A seven-point program of social welfare and another seven-point program of personnel practices were adopted, and the National Coordinating Committee of Rank and File Groups in Social Work was formed to further the objectives set down in these programs. The Committee was expected to co-ordinate the work of some 40 existing groups, to form organizations in areas where there was none, and to provide its constituency with educational material on questions of social welfare, personnel problems, and so on.[2]

At the time the Committee was organized, it was thought of as a transitional step towards an inclusive national membership association for social work employes. In June, 1935, the Committee adopted a proposal for such a membership association and authorized the appointment of persons to draft a constitution. In preparation for taking this step, these representatives were forced to consider two important factors. Although there were many common elements that united the rank-and-file groups, their diversity in composition, aims, and methods was still so great, in the estimation of the representatives, that it precluded the immediate possibility of a strong national membership association. Several

[1] Fisher, Jacob, "Trade Unionism in Social Work," in Social Work Year Book, 1937, pp. 502–505.
[2] *Idem*, The Rank and File Movement in Social Work, 1931–1936. New York School of Social Work, 1936, pp. 36–38.

groups, moreover, were found to be already in process of seeking affiliation with the American Federation of Labor. Since local charters could be obtained so much more easily by the individual groups than could a charter for a country-wide membership association, representatives of the National Coordinating Committee, who had continuously favored strengthening relations with labor, believed that the difficulty of obtaining a national charter was a further reason against forming such an association.

When, therefore, delegates from 29 organizations met in February, 1936, for a second convention, they did not form an association of individual members. They created, instead, the National Coordinating Committee of Social Service Employe Groups, to provide a medium for co-operation among employe groups on issues of an economic, social welfare, or professional nature.

Since that time, events within the labor movement have completely altered plans for the future of the National Coordinating Committee. During 1936 and part of 1937 several groups of employes of public agencies obtained charters as lodges of the American Federation of State, County, and Municipal Employees, an affiliate of the American Federation of Labor, while unions of private agency employes in New York and Chicago were chartered as independent locals of the American Federation of Labor.

In June, 1937, the Committee for Industrial Organization, which a year later was to become the Congress of Industrial Organizations (CIO), created an international union known as the United Office and Professional Workers of America. To it the groups of private agency workers in New York and Chicago at once shifted their allegiance, since the Committee for Industrial Organization seemed to be more interested in "white collar" and professional workers and to offer more guidance, while its program of social legislation appeared more in keeping with national needs as social workers knew them. As the United Office and Professional Workers of America grew in size, seven divisions were formed, corresponding roughly to those occupations in which its members were employed. One of these is the Social Service Division, popularly designated as the Social Service Employees Union. By 1941 some 3,200 workers in private agencies in 18 cities, comprising as many "locals," constituted the membership of the Social Service Division.[1]

Almost immediately after making provision for privately employed office and professional persons, the CIO established another union—the State, County, and Municipal Workers of America—for the purpose of organizing government employes. In 1940 the National Welfare Division was set up within this union in order to provide an agency through which social service workers might more readily co-ordinate their efforts with those of the Social Service Division and with older social work organizations. Nearly 15,000 public assistance workers were reported to be members of this union by 1941. They constituted 39 "locals," situated in 26 cities.[2]

It should be constantly borne in mind that both of these international unions are industrial in character: they are composed of maintenance and clerical workers, as well as of professional employes. The number of their members who

---

[1] Bancroft, Frank C., "Trade Unionism in Social Work," in Social Work Year Book, 1941, pp. 560–561.
[2] Ibid., p. 560.

would customarily be designated as social workers is not known.

Because of the emergence of international trade unions with which social service employes could be affiliated, the National Coordinating Committee decided in May, 1937, that it had fulfilled its function and consequently dissolved. It recommended, however, that a committee composed of representatives of unions in both the public and the private fields, now known as the Joint Committee of Trade Unions in Social Work, be responsible for an annual program at the National Conference of Social Work, and that the magazine, Social Work Today, be incorporated as an independent venture, which should seek the endorsement and support of unions of employes of both official and voluntary agencies.

No comprehensive understanding of the rise of trade union activity in social work is possible without recognition of the fact that the last decade witnessed a growing interest in the labor movement on the part of "white collar" and professionally employed persons in many occupations throughout the country. This interest had its inception, in considerable part, in the financial depression, which subjected these groups to great economic strain and insecurity. To thousands of persons who had never before considered themselves as "laborers" or shown interest in the problems of industrial and agricultural workers, the labor movement came to be regarded as the agency most capable of dealing with the social and economic maladjustments of the United States. The Interprofessional Association, which was created as a rallying point for these very persons and occupational groups, stated its purpose as follows:

1. To organize professional workers in recognition of their common interest with industrial workers and farmers for the promotion of an adequate and inclusive program of unemployment insurance and of other forms of social insurance against economic insecurity.

2. To promote interprofessional co-operation for the economic protection of professional workers in relationship with the labor movement, and for their increasing enlightenment on the issues involved in the growing demand of the American people for economical [*sic*] and social security.[1]

Trade unionism in social work was but one manifestation of a general trend. Many social service employes found, in the basic philosophy of the labor movement, fundamental principles to which they could subscribe; in its methods of exerting pressure through lobbying, the picket line, and stoppage of work, they found tools which they could use. Both the principles and methods of trade unionism have been interpreted in a manner designed to achieve effective action within the specialized field of social service. Thus, the State, County, and Municipal Workers of America have been primarily concerned with support of the merit system, achievement of collective bargaining rights, and co-operation with all organized labor in behalf of more adequately financed and professionally administered programs of public welfare. The union has consistently maintained—writes Frank C. Bancroft, managing editor of Social Work Today —that high professional and technical standards, security of tenure, and adequate remuneration for official employes are in the public interest.[2]

[1] Interprofessional Association for Social Insurance, Purpose and Program. New York, 1935, p. 1.
[2] "Trade Unionism in Social Work," in Social Work Year Book, 1941, p. 561.

Meanwhile the Social Service Employees Union has contended that private social work will be, for some time to come, an integral part of essential social service, and that the obligation of boards of trustees extends to employes as well as to the community generally. It has insisted that the welfare of clients, of workers, and of the community is interrelated, and has opposed contraction of private services while public ones are inadequately developed to meet social needs.

In an effort to raise or at least to maintain salaries and to improve working conditions for employes, and to increase or maintain the level of relief for clients, both unions have engaged—although sparingly and judiciously, the members believe—in the use of pressure tactics. Philadelphia and New York, for example, have viewed in recent years stoppage of work or the picket line or both applied to particular agencies; while St. Louis has seen the strength of the organized labor movement of that city placed at the disposal of the Social Service Employees Union. Under the caption Social Work Democracy in Action, Social Work Today has set forth the issues involved in those cities as analyzed by union members: the right to assemble freely, the right to negotiate and to bargain collectively, the right of employes to participate in the formulation of policies for the agency.[1]

The most widely known campaign in which a social work trade union has engaged was that conducted in 1940 in California as a "protest against drastically lowered relief levels in that state and against increased political manipulation of personnel."[2] For its opposition to measures inter-

[1] December, 1940, pp. 9–15, 30.
[2] Bancroft, Frank C., "Trade Unionism in Social Work," in Social Work Year Book, 1941, p. 561.

preted as designed by the legislature "to destroy the last vestige of decent social service and personnel practice," the State, County, and Municipal Workers of America won from a state assemblyman the heated statement, "The so-called SCMWA is not really a union, just a racket, a Communist controlled racket."[1] Large numbers of the staff of the Alameda County State Relief Administration were summarily dismissed from their positions; members of the union in several counties were called before the Legislative Committee to Investigate Relief; several staff workers of the Stockton County State Relief Administration were tried on charges of contempt, convicted, and sentenced to one year in jail and a $500 fine.

Writing in 1941, Frank C. Bancroft was able to report that a number of the larger locals of social service employes has passed from the status of loosely knit employe groups to that of mature trade unions.[2] Only in the great metropolitan centers of the country and on the Pacific Coast, however, has the trade union movement penetrated social work to any considerable degree. What its future will be is still unknown. To a person like John A. Fitch, "there is more in common between social worker and industrial worker than either has, until recently, thought possible."[3] In a carefully reasoned article, Professor Fitch reminds his readers that:

Any social worker worth his salt is interested in three kinds of security: for himself and his dependents against the hazards

[1] "Professional Values and County Jails," in Social Work Today, June–July, 1940, pp. 15, 30. See also Carey McWilliams' Unmet Needs of Agricultural Workers on pp. 16–17 of the same issue of that periodical.
[2] "Trade Unionism in Social Work," in Social Work Year Book, 1941, p. 563.
[3] "Security in Social Work," in Survey Midmonthly, August, 1938, p. 260.

of low income and unemployment; for himself and his brethren against invasions of their status as members of a profession; for all mankind against forces threatening human personality in every form—economic, political, cultural. . . . It follows from this not only that a union is a fit instrument for the social worker in the defense of his rights and the advancement of his interests, but that affiliation with the labor movement as a whole is appropriate and desirable for him.[1]

NUMBER OF SOCIAL WORKERS

More definite information than formerly is now available concerning the number of persons engaged in social work. The profession, however, is so extensive in scope and its limits are so undefined that difficulty is frequently encountered in determining whether those in certain types of occupations should be classified as social workers or not.

Prior to 1930 the federal census had grouped together "religious, charity and welfare workers." Consequently, statistics obtainable from that source were of little value in determining the number of social workers. In 1930, however, "social and welfare workers" were allotted a separate classification. This step, achieved through the vigilance of the American Association of Social Workers, has been of great value. The question of accuracy of enumeration is always raised in connection with census figures. It is quite possible that some persons designate themselves as social workers even when they have no valid claim to the use of the term. One may presume, however, that with the aid of 76 social work titles which the Bureau of the Census selected for inclusion in its 1930 Index of Occupations, and with the assistance which many social workers gave enumerators in

[1] *Ibid.*, pp. 259, 260.

rightly classifying their occupation, the count for that profession may well have been as correct as it was for most other occupations.

The 1930 census recorded 31,241 "social and welfare workers." Although that figure may include some who were not social workers, it does not include the entire social work group. Public health nurses, of whom the National Organization for Public Health Nursing counted 15,865 in 1931, were classified by the Bureau of the Census with other graduate nurses, although their work is closely related to, if not a part of, social work. All gainfully employed persons in the Young Men's Christian Association, Young Women's Christian Association, Young Men's Hebrew Association, Young Women's Hebrew Association, Salvation Army, church organizations, religious sisterhoods, and the like were counted as religious workers. Within this group, however, are many genuine social work positions. In another census category, "keepers of charitable and penal institutions," there were probably some social workers. The number is not likely to be very large, as the heads of all children's institutions except day nurseries were classified as social or welfare workers. The census category "probation and truant officers," however, consists chiefly of probation and parole officers, and since they are generally considered to be social workers, this item of 4,270—which is probably too small—should be included. Among "county agents, farm demonstrators, etc.," also there was in 1930, as today, an important group of rural social workers. They are the county agents working with rural boys' and girls' clubs, and the home demonstration agents employed in the agricultural extension services which are conducted jointly by the federal Department of Agriculture and the state agricultural colleges. Perhaps 2,000 of the 5,597 persons in this census group should be considered social workers. Ralph G. Hurlin, who carefully examined the census statistics, concluded that when allowance was made for the numbers in the various fields just mentioned, it is safe to estimate that in 1930 there were 40,000, and perhaps 42,500, social workers. This does not include the 15,000 or 16,000 public health nurses. Neither does it include volunteer workers.[1]

In preparation for the 1940 census, the category of "social and welfare workers" was appreciably enlarged to include, among 108 titles, executive and technical positions in the four young men's and young women's associations, heads of day nurseries, probation and parole officers, and juvenile and truant officers. The 1930 categories of "religious workers," "keepers of charitable and penal institutions," and "probation and truant officers" have been dropped, at least from the initial reports issued by the Bureau of the Census. Some of the persons formerly counted in the first and second categories and supposedly all of those in the third category have been transferred to "social and welfare workers." "County agents" have been classified in 1940 with teachers.

The tabulation of the census figures for 1940 shows a total of 69,677 "social and welfare workers" who reported themselves as employed. In addition 2,851 social workers, not employed at the time of registration, were counted. These two groups constitute an increase of more than 41,000 over the number thus classified for 1930. If, how-

[1] The Number and Distribution of Social Workers in the United States. Russell Sage Foundation, New York, 1933, pp. 3–7.

ever, the estimate of 40,000, the base of which is fairly comparable with the 1940 figures, is used for the earlier year instead of the census figure of 31,241, the increase indicated by the census figures is under 33,000.

As public social work underwent its greatest expansion in American history during the decade of the 1930's, there was renewed speculation about the total number of social workers. It was believed that the number in private agencies had remained approximately the same. The personnel of public agencies providing general relief had been enlarged during the middle years of the depression with dizzying rapidity. Later some decrease had occurred, but then staffs were being built up in divisions of public agencies whose functions had been created or augmented as the result of the Social Security Act of 1935 and subsequent legislation. Hence, it was thought by some that the federal census might show a figure as high as 100,000. No such result was disclosed.

Because the census figures did not become available until May, 1942, there has, as yet, been little opportunity for social work statisticians to examine them or attempt to evaluate their accuracy. One check, however, awaited immediate use. It is that of the count of social workers in Rhode Island in 1941, made by the Rhode Island chapter of the American Association of Social Workers.[1] According to this record, 312 men and 531 women were employed in social work positions in the state, whereas the federal census reported 161 men and 379 women. Thus the Bureau of the Census registered 36 per cent fewer social workers in Rhode Island than did the chapter, which made strenuous effort to "hunt out"

---

[1] Myers, Dorothy W., "Census of Social Workers in Rhode Island: 1941," in The Compass, November, 1941, pp. 13–14.

social workers in the positions listed under social work titles by the Bureau. It may perhaps be concluded that the Rhode Island survey was somewhat too inclusive; that the federal census was not inclusive enough.

Existing data concerning social work positions in a considerable number of state and local public welfare departments indicate, additionally, that the census results may be too low. Figures for these departments in many states are so large that, were figures for private and other public social workers also available, the totals would undoubtedly exceed those of the federal census.

It should be borne in mind, furthermore, that even in 1940 some groups escaped count as social workers. Within the Catholic religious orders of the United States, there must be at least 3,500 sisters performing tasks that could properly be classified as social work, who were probably not included.[1] County agents, and perhaps heads of institutions for adults, were counted elsewhere. Public health nurses, of whom there were some 23,700[2] in 1940, were appropriately included with graduate nurses.

Regardless of final judgment about the accuracy of the census figures, the count was undoubtedly complete enough to justify attention to certain trends indicated by it. For this purpose, our analysis is confined to the figures for employed social workers. The first of these important tendencies is the increasing percentage of men in social work. The

[1] Hurlin, Ralph G., "An Occupational Census of the Catholic Sisterhoods in the United States," in Twentieth National Conference of Catholic Charities, 1934, p. 375.

[2] Figure, as of January 1, 1940, reported by the U.S. Public Health Service for active public health nurses in the U.S., Hawaii, and Alaska, in Public Health Nursing, January, 1941, p. 21.

1930 census reported that 27 per cent of all social workers were men. The percentage had risen in 1940 to 36, the inclusion of probation and parole officers in the latter year being partly responsible for the marked increase. As shown in Table 7, the ratio differs widely from state to state. It was lowest in 1940 in Alabama, which reported a percentage of 18. In seven other southern states, the ratio did not exceed 25. It was highest in Wyoming, the Dakotas, and West Virginia, which had percentages of from 46 to 48. In New York 39 per cent of the 14,633 social workers were men.

Until the Selective Service Act began to play havoc with occupational choice, men were continuously assuming a more important role numerically in social work. In responsible executive positions they held office out of all proportion to their numbers. The growth of public welfare had done much to attract them to social work. The Rhode Island count revealed that 70 per cent of the 312 men social workers in that state were in public agencies, which include probation and parole. Generally in protective and correctional work, men have outnumbered women. In group-work and recreational agencies the two sexes have been probably almost equally divided. In most types of case work, on the other hand, women have always been decidedly more numerous than men. In such fields as medical and psychiatric social work, visiting teaching, and day nurseries, practically no positions have ever been held by men.

Table 7 reveals that each of five large, heavily populated, and highly industrialized states reported more than 4,000 social workers. Collectively these five states had half the social workers in the entire nation. Eight states, at the other extreme, that are either sparsely populated or very small,

TABLE 7.—EMPLOYED SOCIAL WORKERS IN 1940, AS RE-
CORDED BY THE BUREAU OF THE CENSUS,
BY STATES AND SEX

States grouped by number of social workers	Total	Men		Women	
		Number	Per cent	Number	Per cent
More than 4,000					
New York	14,633	5,705	39	8,928	61
California	6,022	2,039	34	3,983	66
Pennsylvania	5,939	2,167	37	3,772	63
Illinois	4,362	1,495	34	2,867	66
Ohio	4,012	1,526	38	2,486	62
2,000 to 4,000					
Massachusetts	3,070	1,232	40	1,838	60
Michigan	2,798	1,131	40	1,667	60
New Jersey	2,560	1,105	43	1,455	57
1,000 to 2,000					
Indiana	1,674	507	30	1,167	70
Minnesota	1,649	581	35	1,068	65
Texas	1,567	565	36	1,002	64
Missouri	1,530	474	31	1,056	69
Wisconsin	1,414	605	43	809	57
Connecticut	1,145	365	32	780	68
Louisiana	1,056	230	22	826	78
500 to 1,000					
Maryland	969	228	24	741	76
Washington	964	328	34	636	66
Kentucky	867	337	39	530	61
Virginia	865	219	25	646	75
Tennessee	850	199	23	651	77
Iowa	838	321	38	517	62
North Carolina	827	267	32	560	68
Oklahoma	798	229	29	569	71
Georgia	758	189	25	569	75
Kansas	755	248	33	507	67
Florida	736	165	22	571	78
West Virginia	619	289	47	330	53
Dist. of Columbia	607	191	32	416	68
Colorado	599	195	33	404	67
Rhode Island	540	161	30	379	70
Alabama	514	91	18	423	82
Nebraska	507	195	39	312	61

TABLE 7 (*Continued*)

States grouped by number of social workers	Total	Men		Women	
		Number	Per cent	Number	Per cent
200 to 500					
South Carolina	427	88	21	339	79
Oregon	416	124	30	292	70
Maine	322	118	37	204	63
Utah	282	116	41	166	59
Mississippi	281	79	28	202	72
Arkansas	278	89	32	189	68
New Hampshire	226	87	39	139	61
Arizona	213	94	44	119	56
North Dakota	211	97	46	114	54
Fewer than 200					
Montana	196	84	43	112	57
South Dakota	169	80	47	89	53
Delaware	153	44	29	109	71
Idaho	135	62	46	73	54
New Mexico	132	52	39	80	61
Vermont	87	26	30	61	70
Wyoming	73	35	48	38	52
Nevada	32	14	44	18	56
Total	69,677	24,868	36	44,809	64

had fewer than 200 social workers each and a total under
1,000.

Absolute figures, such as these, have some value and are
of considerable interest. When they are viewed in comparison with population, however, they assume greatly added
significance. Table 8, which is concerned with ratio of population to social workers, indicates that New York has not
only the largest absolute, but also the largest relative, number of social workers. It is the only state with fewer than
1,000 persons in the total population to each social worker.
Had the District of Columbia been included in this table, it
would have shown the next highest ratio of population per

social worker—1,092—but it may be disregarded here, since its favorable ratio results from the residence in Washington of many social workers employed by federal agen-

TABLE 8.—POPULATION PER EMPLOYED SOCIAL WORKER IN 1940, ACCORDING TO BUREAU OF THE CENSUS FIGURES, BY STATES

Rank	State	Persons per social worker	Rank	State	Persons per social worker
1	New York	921	26	Oregon	2,619
			27	Maine	2,631
2	California	1,147	28	Montana	2,854
3	Rhode Island	1,321	29	Oklahoma	2,928
4	Massachusetts	1,406			
5	Connecticut	1,493	30	Iowa	3,029
6	New Jersey	1,625	31	North Dakota	3,042
7	Pennsylvania	1,667	32	West Virginia	3,073
8	Minnesota	1,693	33	Virginia	3,096
9	Ohio	1,722	34	Kentucky	3,282
10	Delaware	1,742	35	Tennessee	3,430
11	Washington	1,801	36	Wyoming	3,435
12	Illinois	1,810	37	Nevada	3,445
13	Colorado	1,875	38	South Dakota	3,805
14	Michigan	1,879	39	Idaho	3,888
15	Maryland	1,880			
16	Utah	1,951	40	New Mexico	4,029
			41	Texas	4,094
17	Indiana	2,048	42	Georgia	4,121
18	New Hampshire	2,175	43	Vermont	4,129
19	Wisconsin	2,219	44	North Carolina	4,319
20	Louisiana	2,239	45	South Carolina	4,449
21	Arizona	2,344			
22	Kansas	2,385	46	Alabama	5,512
23	Missouri	2,474			
24	Florida	2,578	47	Arkansas	7,012
25	Nebraska	2,595	48	Mississippi	7,772

cies that serve the whole nation. California, among the states, takes second place; diminutive Rhode Island, that held thirtieth place in Table 7, moves into third place; then follow four other states on the eastern seaboard. Interestingly enough, the relatively young but progressive Minnesota occupies the eighth place; Washington, another young state, the eleventh; Colorado, thirteenth; and Utah, sixteenth. In the first 16 states, there are fewer than 2,000 persons to each social worker. The median figure for the 48 states is 2,586, but the average for the United States, heavily influenced by the larger states, is only 1,890 persons per social worker.

At the bottom of Table 8 are nine states with the distinctly unfavorable ratio of more than 4,000 persons to each social worker. Seven are southern states; one is Vermont, conservative and slow-moving; one is New Mexico, with its half million population predominantly of Spanish and Indian heritage. The sparsely settled Mountain states, most of which were in the last group in Table 7, have moved up in Table 8. Montana, in ratio of social workers to population, rises to twenty-eighth position; Nevada that reported only seven social workers in 1930 and 32 in 1940, by virtue of its mere 110,000 population moves to thirty-seventh place in relation of persons to social workers.

Distribution of social workers within state boundaries is also instructive. Table 9 shows the division of all social workers and also of all persons into three population areas: cities of over 100,000 persons; "urban" areas of between 2,500 and 100,000 population; and rural non-farm and farm areas. Caution is essential in interpreting these figures. The Bureau of the Census enumerates persons by residence rather than by place of occupation. As a result, the many social workers who live in suburban areas but are employed in large cities tend to diminish the figure for the large places. In respect to the ratio of population to social workers in

TABLE 9.—DISTRIBUTION OF EMPLOYED SOCIAL WORKERS AND OF POPULATION IN URBAN AND RURAL AREAS, BY STATES

Geographic division and state	Population per social worker, entire state	Cities of over 100,000 population			Places of from 2,500 to 100,000 population			Places of less than 2,500 population		
		Social workers, per cent of total in state	Population per cent of total in state	Population per social worker	Social workers, per cent of total in state	Population per cent of total in state	Population per social worker	Social workers, per cent of total in state	Population per cent of total in state	Population per social worker
New England										
Maine	2,631	—	—	—	62.7	40.5	1,698	37.3	59.5	4,201
New Hampshire	2,175	—	—	—	75.2	57.6	1,666	24.8	42.4	3,720
Vermont	4,129	—	—	—	69.0	34.3	2,054	31.0	65.7	8,740
Massachusetts	1,406	52.1	38.3	1,035	42.3	51.1	1,698	5.6	10.6	2,643
Rhode Island	1,321	54.1	35.5	868	41.3	56.1	1,793	4.6	8.4	2,399
Connecticut	1,493	37.8	27.7	1,095	34.1	40.0	1,754	28.1	32.3	1,711
Middle Atlantic										
New York	921	75.6	66.3	808	14.2	16.5	1,071	10.2	17.2	1,548
New Jersey	1,625	33.7	29.4	1,418	52.1	52.2	1,629	14.2	18.4	2,097
Pennsylvania	1,667	46.1	30.0	1,086	39.4	36.5	1,545	14.5	33.5	3,835
East North Central										
Ohio	1,722	54.4	38.4	1,217	33.5	28.4	1,459	12.1	33.2	4,702
Indiana	2,048	38.4	21.0	1,117	39.3	34.1	1,777	22.3	44.9	4,129
Illinois	1,810	63.5	44.4	1,265	29.6	29.2	1,789	6.9	26.4	6,890
Michigan	1,879	49.6	36.9	1,396	35.6	28.8	1,523	14.8	34.3	4,351
Wisconsin	2,219	29.4	18.7	1,412	56.1	34.8	1,377	14.5	46.5	7,114
West North Central										
Minnesota	1,693	70.3	31.6	760	18.4	18.2	1,674	11.3	50.2	7,539
Iowa	3,029	21.2	6.3	898	66.0	36.4	1,672	12.8	57.3	13,589
Missouri	2,474	57.4	32.1	1,384	29.1	19.7	1,675	13.5	48.2	8,811
North Dakota	3,042	—	—	—	58.3	20.6	1,073	41.7	79.4	5,796
South Dakota	3,805	—	—	—	59.2	24.6	1,581	40.8	75.4	7,027
Nebraska	2,595	34.1	17.0	1,294	43.4	22.1	1,320	22.5	60.9	7,032

Delaware	1,742	62.8	42.2	1,172	12.4	10.1	1,417	24.8	47.7	3,344
Maryland	1,880	58.0	47.7	1,529	13.2	12.1	1,729	28.8	40.7	2,656
Dist. of Columbia	1,092	100.0	100.0	1,092	—	—	—	—	—	—
Virginia	3,096	34.4	12.6	1,132	36.1	22.7	1,946	29.5	64.7	6,796
West Virginia	3,073	—	—	—	56.5	28.1	1,527	43.5	71.9	5,084
North Carolina	4,319	6.6	2.8	1,835	55.9	24.5	1,890	37.5	72.7	8,379
South Carolina	4,449	—	—	—	66.0	24.5	1,653	34.0	75.5	9,888
Georgia	4,121	26.0	9.7	1,534	46.2	24.7	2,204	27.8	65.6	9,715
Florida	2,578	30.3	23.9	2,034	46.7	31.2	1,721	23.0	44.9	5,039
East South Central										
Kentucky	3,282	26.1	11.2	1,412	28.7	18.6	2,130	45.2	70.2	5,093
Tennessee	3,430	52.9	24.0	1,556	18.7	11.2	2,057	28.4	64.8	7,837
Alabama	5,512	20.2	9.4	2,573	52.5	20.8	2,179	27.3	69.8	14,122
Mississippi	7,772	—	—	—	64.4	19.8	2,392	35.6	80.2	17,509
West South Central										
Arkansas	7,012	—	—	—	69.8	22.2	2,226	30.2	77.8	18,065
Louisiana	2,239	35.1	20.9	1,337	33.4	20.6	1,376	31.5	58.5	4,154
Oklahoma	2,928	30.2	14.8	1,438	46.4	22.8	1,441	23.4	62.4	7,790
Texas	4,094	35.1	17.3	2,020	44.3	28.1	2,595	20.6	54.6	10,847
Mountain										
Montana	2,854	—	—	—	70.9	37.8	1,522	29.1	62.2	6,104
Idaho	3,888	—	—	—	78.5	33.7	1,667	21.5	66.3	12,006
Wyoming	3,435	—	—	—	71.2	37.3	1,800	28.8	62.7	7,484
Colorado	1,875	43.3	28.7	1,245	33.7	23.9	1,328	23.0	47.4	3,859
New Mexico	4,029	—	—	—	73.5	33.2	1,819	26.5	66.8	10,155
Arizona	2,344	—	—	—	59.2	34.8	1,381	40.8	65.2	3,739
Utah	1,951	45.7	27.2	1,162	34.8	28.3	1,587	19.5	44.5	4,451
Nevada	3,445	—	—	—	59.4	39.3	2,278	40.6	60.7	5,150
Pacific										
Washington	1,801	53.0	34.5	1,174	27.5	18.6	1,216	19.5	46.9	4,331
Oregon	2,619	58.4	28.0	1,257	26.5	20.8	2,057	15.1	51.2	8,857
California	1,147	52.9	42.2	915	34.1	28.8	968	13.0	29.0	2,564
Total	1,890	50.6	28.8	1,078	33.4	27.7	1,566	16.0	43.5	5,125

cities of over 100,000 New York City, for example, took tenth place in 1940. Had scores of social workers who commute daily from Westchester County and from New Jersey been counted by place of occupation, it is probable that New York City would have been higher in the list of big cities. Cambridge, Massachusetts, to cite another example, stood first in ratio of social workers to population, while Boston stood eleventh. Many Boston social workers undoubtedly maintain residence across the Charles River in Cambridge.

Conversely, some social workers live in an urban setting and go daily to work in smaller places, or are employed by agencies whose offices are in a city but whose program is statewide or countywide. Thus investigation would probably show that a large proportion of persons providing rural services lived in places of more than 2,500 population. Every state capital and many county seats have varying numbers of social workers who render little or no direct service to the municipality in which their offices are located.

In spite of these difficulties in interpreting Table 9, the conclusion is inescapable that social work is a highly urbanized profession. Eighty-four per cent of all social workers were reported to be in "urban" areas, as the term is used by the Bureau of the Census, although such areas accounted for only 57 per cent of the population. In the 92 cities of over 100,000 alone, which had 29 per cent of the population, were registered 51 per cent of all social workers. The state which had the greatest proportion of social workers in large cities was New York. Its seven cities of over 100,000 had 76 per cent of the entire social work personnel of the state, but they had 66 per cent of the state's population. North Carolina, which is largely rural, was at the other extreme.

Only 7 per cent of its social workers and 3 per cent of its population were within Charlotte, its one city which has reached the 100,000 mark. In every state that has one or more big cities, the percentage of social workers in such places exceeded their percentage of the population, and ratios of population per social worker were uniformly low.

In communities of over 2,500 but under 100,000, the percentage of social workers still exceeded that of population, except in Massachusetts, Rhode Island, Connecticut, and New York. Fifteen states have no city of the first category. In such states, therefore, smaller cities play a relatively more important role, and the percentage of social workers averaged 34 points above the percentage of population.

Although 44 per cent of all the people of the United States at present live in places under 2,500, only 16 per cent of the social workers were registered as living there. As has been noted above, this figure probably does not include all persons rendering service to the rural areas. At best, however, the proportion of social workers engaged in the up-building of country life is small. In no state was the percentage of rural social workers as large as the percentage of rural population. The situation was most unfavorable in Arkansas where the percentage of rural population was 48 points greater than that of social workers and where there was but one social worker for each 18,000 persons. The ratio of rural population per social worker was found to be most favorable in New York, Connecticut, New Jersey, Rhode Island, California, Massachusetts, and Maryland, in that order. These seven states are the only ones with fewer than 3,000 persons per social worker in rural areas.

Not until recently has there been general awareness that

some of the rural areas—with their tenant farmers, share-croppers, illiteracy, and high incidence of disease—are quite as much in need of social services as are highly industrialized cities. The New Deal particularly has done much to enlarge and strengthen this awareness and to foster extension of rural social services. Were census figures for the number of rural social workers in 1930 available, an appreciable increase during the decade would undoubtedly be noted, but social welfare programs for villages and farms are still in their initial stages.

Before bringing this section to a close brief reference should be made to the number of social workers as compared with the number of persons in other professional groups. Some 70,000 social workers appear very few when contrasted with more than a million teachers, 356,000 graduate and student nurses, 245,000 professional engineers, 178,000 lawyers and judges, 165,000 physicians, and 133,000 clergymen. They are more than twice as numerous as librarians, however, and more than three times as numerous as architects, according to Census Bureau figures. When rate of growth in the several professions between 1930 and 1940 is considered, the picture changes. Clergymen and architects declined 10 per cent in number, dentists 3 per cent, and teachers 1 per cent. Most other professions, except nursing and social work, made modest gains of from 7 to 11 per cent. Nurses increased by 21 per cent; social workers probably increased by at least 75 to 80 per cent.

DEMAND FOR SOCIAL WORKERS

The number of social workers and the demand for their services are inextricably linked. It is impossible to discuss one of these questions without considering the other. It is almost as difficult, however, to obtain any comprehensive picture of demand as it formerly was to determine the number of social workers. There are various reasons for this difficulty. One of them is the youth of the profession. Personnel accounting is as yet little developed. There are no statistical data relating to demand and supply comparable, for instance, to those published by the National Education Association.

Another reason for the difficulty in determining the relation between supply and demand lies in the failure of many people, even social workers themselves, to differentiate between the need for social work and the demand for it. Demand implies desire coupled with the ability to pay. Need is undoubtedly great; about demand there is more question. Does society consider social work necessary enough to pay for it? Society as now organized is evidently not able or willing to pay for all it needs, and for such work as it does require, salaries are often so small that they discourage many well-educated people from entering the profession. But these distressing facts are true not only for social work but for many other occupations. Society does not demand all the services which it needs from any professional group. The National Health Conference held in Washington in 1938 revealed that a startling percentage of the people receive no medical or dental attention whatever during the course of a year.[1] Although lawyers seem overabundant in the large cities, there is apparently a great amount of legal work that the public needs and which

[1] Proceedings of the National Health Conference, July 18, 19, 20, 1938, Washington, D.C. Government Printing Office, Washington, 1938.

would be done if society knew how to obtain efficient and inexpensive service.

Although concrete information about demand for social workers is inadequate, certain recent trends are illuminating. Public social work developed, as has already been noted, with unprecedented rapidity during the last decade. During the early years of the depression, the demand for trained persons was so great that the available supply was notably insufficient. Large numbers of professional social workers left private agencies, either temporarily or permanently, to staff public agencies with administrative and supervisory personnel. Persons who in many instances had had only small amounts of training and experience were immediately placed in positions of much greater responsibility than the private agencies would have awarded them. No possibility existed, however, of obtaining any considerable number of persons with even a minimum of training or experience for the thousands of positions of investigator. Hence staffs had to be recruited hastily, often in large part from the rolls of unemployed persons. The dual task of administering vast relief programs and of creating a functioning staff largely from raw recruits proceeded as best it could.

Weeding out of the most unfit workers proceeded rapidly at first; training on the job was provided with varying degrees of efficiency; many employes who showed aptitude for and interest in social work enrolled in evening courses in schools of social work or universities; federal and state scholarships made it possible for some selected persons to obtain a quarter or semester of resident professional training; merit system examinations proved an incentive for workers "to qualify" for permanent appointments.

During the years in which this process of assimilation was going on, several new schools of social work were being established, and many of the graduates both of the new and the older schools immediately entered public welfare rather than private agencies. Thus the schools began the process of directly supplying the governmental agencies with a professionally trained personnel.

From the chaos of the early depression period have come permanent departments of public welfare, greatly expanded social services, and a much increased personnel. By 1940 the social work scene appeared to be again largely stabilized, but on a level numerically far in advance of that a decade earlier. Conditions in Europe, however, pointed to the fact that stabilization was not likely to continue. Even before 1940 several new or existent agencies had undertaken programs of assistance to refugees from Nazi-controlled countries. The National Refugee Service, the largest of the new agencies and the one with which many of the others became affiliated, was already staggering under a case load of almost incredible size. The American Red Cross, too, was undertaking expansion of staff.

As the Selective Service Act of September, 1940, scattered the country with army camps and we entered the period of "unlimited national emergency," organization for service to the armed forces and workers in war industries, and for civilian defense began making emphatic demands upon social workers. Expansion in the Red Cross gained great momentum. By July, 1942, J. Blaine Gwin, director of employment, reported that nearly 500 men were engaged in Red Cross camp and club work, 200 women were doing medical social work in hospitals, more than 900 persons were executive secretaries of chapters, and approximately 450 were home-service workers in chapters. Not counting executives at the national headquarters and in the "area offices," some of whom were social workers, but including 350 men and women in training who were awaiting assignment, the Red Cross was employing, as of that date, almost 2,500 persons in social work positions.

The United Service Organizations, composed of the six private agencies—National Travelers Aid Association, National Catholic Community Service, Jewish Welfare Board, Salvation Army, Young Men's Christian Associations, and Young Women's Christian Associations—undertook the task of providing recreational and social service facilities in military and industrial defense communities. By July, 1942, the USO was operating, in 45 states and 11 areas or bases outside continental United States, 528 clubs, 66 travelers aid services, 56 lounge services for troops in transit, and 19 mobile services.[1] The professional staff, exclusive of persons employed in the central office, numbered 1,552 and was still continuing to grow rapidly. How many of these persons would be classified by training as social workers was not known, but the proportion was large, and it can be said that, in general, most of them occupied social work positions.

The first countrywide effort to bring social welfare agencies generally to the aid of national defense was instituted late in 1940, when the Federal Security Administrator was named co-ordinator of all health, medical, welfare, nutri-

[1] United Service Organizations, USO Local Operations and Local Professional Staff as of July 6, 1942. Weekly mimeographed statistical statement.

tional, recreational, and some educational facilities that affected the national defense. Subsequently, the Office of Defense Health and Welfare Services was created within the Federal Security Agency for the purpose of performing this task. The central office in Washington and the 12 regional offices attempt to rally both the public and private welfare resources of specific areas to meet needs arising from war-industry and defense conditions, and to co-ordinate such services for the entire nation during the emergency.

As yet, the Office has created no considerable demand for social workers. Although its function may be considered social work in the broadest sense, part of its program is in the hands of physicians and nutritionists. The work of the Family Security Committee, Social Protection Committee, and Community Organization Committee, however, falls within the core of social work. Because most of the undertakings of the Office are carried on by voluntary committees drawn from established agencies, the staff is small. In October, 1941, the professional personnel numbered 198.[1] It is the function of the staff to assume responsibility for general planning and supervision, and to make the services of health and welfare consultants available, upon request, to state and local areas. Only in communities where no existing agency has had primary responsibility does it undertake direct operation of work.

Civilian defense, organization for which was begun in the spring of 1941, has evolved into a nationwide movement under the direction of the federal Office of Civilian

[1] Cosgrove, Elizabeth, and Hillyer, Cecile, Public Welfare Positions in the Federal Service. Mimeographed summary of this report prepared at the request of the Director of Defense Health and Welfare Services, p. 8.

Defense. Since the vast program is primarily concerned with protection of life and property in an emergency, it falls outside the field of social work. In the national office, however, there were 24 public welfare positions in October, 1941. It was the function of persons in these positions to advise state and local officials and private agencies about the goal of the civilian defense program and how to establish and maintain civilian participation.

In local communities throughout the United States, the program of civilian defense has had vast implications for departments of public welfare and private social agencies. A recent article by William Hodson, Commissioner of Welfare and also Emergency Welfare Administrator in New York City, illustrates how extensive is the planning that must be made for providing social services under enemy attack.[1]

Mr. Hodson reports that the Department of Welfare has set up 65 Emergency Welfare Centers in New York City, staffed with experienced workers, and has co-ordinated all the welfare services that will be available in these centers. Services include advice and information, cash allowances, clothing, temporary and permanent rehousing for persons bombed out of their homes, and so on. Arrangements have been made for communal feeding to the extent of 40,000 meals a day. The Red Cross and Salvation Army are prepared to operate mobile kitchens for street feeding, and the Red Cross has set up more than 700 Emergency Rest Centers to provide food, clothing, and shelter for a few hours.

The emergency welfare staff that will work in the 65 cen-

[1] "The Emergency Welfare Division in Civilian Defense," in The Family, June, 1942, pp. 152–154.

ters in the event of enemy action consists of 2,500 persons: 2,000 regular employes of the Department of Welfare and 500 employes of private agencies. In May, 1942, the Department also had enrolled 150 volunteers referred to it by the Civilian Defense Volunteer Office. After a brief training course, these volunteers were assigned to work in the Department, in order to become familiar with function and operation. In an emergency they would supervise other volunteers. Training and placing of volunteers will supposedly continue as long as they are available and as fast as they can be taken into the Department.

Regardless of the degree of preparation that has been made in various communities, civilian defense has resulted primarily in arranging to co-ordinate welfare resources and to call upon volunteer aid. It has increased the burden of many employed social workers, but it has not appreciably increased their number. In fact, many public assistance agencies have reduced their staffs during the past year, because the heavy employment in war industries has greatly lessened the need for home relief.

Thus far the only effective demand for any considerable group of additional social workers has come from the American Red Cross and the USO. This is surprising to many persons, since there has been much talk of need for a greatly expanded social work personnel. Need has not yet been translated into demand. Enemy attacks upon the United States might quickly lead to desperate efforts to obtain the services of increased numbers of social workers. A long-continued, punitive war that drastically reduced standards of living and destroyed large segments of the economic and social fabric of our culture would probably produce the same results, although more slowly. If maintenance of national morale under war should require constant expansion of the public services, demand would increase. So would it if specific existing areas of service were more intensively cultivated.

One area which formerly received only slight attention but which may undergo rapid and immediate development is that of day centers for small children. Because of the imperative demand for workers in war industries, facilities must be created to free mothers from the necessity of staying at home to care for children of preschool age. Need has long existed for many more social agencies where underprivileged youngsters would be provided with supervised play, education, rest, and food. Centers are now likely to be established, although it is probable that the great majority will not be under social work auspices. Howard W. Hopkirk, executive director of the Child Welfare League of America, has estimated that 200,000 children may receive day care in 1942. Of these, he thinks not more than 50,000 would be supervised by social work agencies. Assuming that there were 250 professional workers in the field of day care before expansion began and that each worker was responsible for overseeing the care of some 60 children, he concludes that 550 additional workers would be required for this quarter of the total estimated need.[1]

Much of the talk about need for an expanded social work personnel has resulted from certain exploratory estimates of "shortages" in social work. "Shortages" may refer either to

[1] Personnel Needs To Be Anticipated in Day Care of Children of Working Mothers. A memorandum submitted by Mr. Hopkirk, February 21, 1942, to Wartime Commission, U.S. Office of Education.

present and prospective vacant positions, or to additional positions that are being or may be created. Since the term has been used, sometimes with one connotation and sometimes with both, very dissimilar figures have been obtained and much general confusion has resulted. In the winter of 1942 the Committee on Community Service Workers of the United States Office of Education's Wartime Commission, and also the Family Security Committee of the Office of Defense Health and Welfare Services, attempted to estimate "shortages" as a basis for a possible congressional grant to subsidize training of social workers during the emergency. In the final report of the Committee on Community Service Workers, a rough estimate of the number of persons who it thought would be needed to replace those leaving social work and to staff new services that might be created reached the staggering total of 12,550.[1]

The Family Security Committee did not estimate future demand for personnel to staff new positions; it did attempt, however, to discover the approximate number of vacant positions in social work agencies in the autumn of 1941.[2] Mary Bateman Novick, who prepared the report of the uncompleted survey, recorded that a "shortage" of only 650 social workers was actually found in the large number of federal, state, and private agencies that responded to the request for information. About 45 per cent of the reported vacancies were in the federal civil service. Applicants for these positions were numerous, but minimum qualifications were rela-

[1] Final Report, April 14, 1942. Typed, pp. 2–3.
[2] Novick, Mary Bateman, Shortages of Qualified Social Welfare Personnel in 1941. Report prepared for the Family Security Committee of the Office of Defense Health and Welfare Services, Washington, March 14, 1942. Mimeographed, pp. 2–3.

tively high. Hence a large proportion failed to meet the requirements either of education or of experience. Another 27 per cent were in state or local public assistance agencies for which reports were submitted. Residence requirements and low salary scales were thought to account for many of these unfilled positions. Private family welfare and child welfare agencies, reporting through the Family Welfare Association of America and the Child Welfare League of America, indicated that only 120 case-work and supervisory positions were unfilled. Only 50 vacancies were found by the United States Public Health Service in social work departments of public and private hospitals. Other fields of social work, including the Red Cross and the USO agencies, were not covered by the report.

It should be borne in mind that a high rate of turnover, particularly in case-work positions, has long characterized social work. When Mr. Hurlin made his examination of employment of professional workers in 207 family welfare agencies, he noted that the rate of turnover in the year 1938 was 22 per cent.[1] Among caseworkers, it rose to 29. In the 203 children's agencies studied by him in 1941, 27 per cent of the 1,458 caseworkers had been with the agency employing them less than one year, and 51 per cent less than three years.[2] The situation was better among the 251 supervisors, but 11 per cent had been with the present agency less than one year and 25 per cent less than three years. Even among heads of agencies 22 per cent had been in the positions then occupied for less than three years.

[1] Employment of New Professional Workers by Private Family Case-Work Agencies in 1938. Russell Sage Foundation, New York, July, 1939. Mimeographed, p. 5.
[2] Material not yet published.

In spite of customarily rapid turnover of staff, the Family Welfare Association of America believes that the interval between loss of staff and replacements is now widening in its member agencies.[1] There is a gradual loss of men to the armed forces, and there are fewer new applicants for jobs. Some women, married to men in the armed forces or to industrial workers who are on the move, are being lost to their employing agencies, if not to social work. The better salaries paid by the Red Cross and USO are drawing workers away from the family welfare societies. Unless the current recruitment program sponsored by the American Association of Schools of Social Work bears early fruit, there is prospect of smaller enrollments in schools of social work in the autumn of 1942.

Dislocation, characteristic of family welfare agencies, is likely to become apparent throughout the field of social work. If the war is long continued, short periods of training will probably be provided for persons who will then assist in social welfare work, either on a voluntary or a paid basis. Should such assistants be utilized extensively, social work would perhaps emerge from the war, as it emerged from the economic depression, with a new body of personnel—a body that would claim the right to be regarded as social workers by virtue of experience rather than of prolonged professional training.

SALARIES

As social work has moved in the direction of professionalism, the attitude has become increasingly widespread that

[1] "F.W.A.A. Information Service," in Highlights, May, 1942, pp. 42–49.

its workers should receive salaries large enough to permit them to maintain a professional standard of living, comparable to that of other groups requiring a similar amount of education and training and sufficient to compensate for the cost of their preparation. Thus far, however, it has seemed to be impossible to translate this ideal extensively into practice.

The relation which exists between social case-work salaries, at least, and the standard of living is very much like the relation between the average worker's wage and the $2,000 income which was estimated in the days before the depression as a necessity for keeping a family of five in decency and comfort. The salary level of the rank-and-file positions in social work is higher than general wages, to be sure, but the discrepancy between it and the standard of living which one would expect a professional person to maintain is almost equally great. Social work salaries are not sufficiently high to provide opportunities for travel, study, and the purchase of books adequate for professional growth and efficiency. This is extremely unfortunate because social workers need every possible enrichment of their experience if they are to have the breadth of judgment and the vision necessary for their very difficult tasks.

The salary situation is also a misfortune from the point of view of professional prestige. In the early days of social work, it was thought unnecessary, if not unethical, that persons who gave their lives to "charity" should receive more than a bare maintenance. But in our social order there is a direct relationship between the income of the individual and the influence which he is able to exert in the community. Because social workers have not been in the well-remunerated class, they have often been seriously handicapped in what they have been able to accomplish.

Sincere efforts, over a period of years, were made to improve the salary situation. Increases occurred, though very gradually, until the economic cataclysm. According to a study made in 1925, the median salary of workers below the grade of supervisor in 132 organizations advanced from $840 in 1913 to $1,220 in 1920, and had reached $1,517 by 1925. It is necessary to bear in mind, however, what had been happening to the purchasing power of the dollar during that period. The cost of living rose sharply from 1915 to 1920, while social workers' salaries moved upward only moderately. As a result, the real value of these salaries dropped. With the decline of prices in 1921 and 1922 salaries gained in value, but the salary curve did not catch up with the cost of living until 1924, and in 1925 was barely above it. In the latter year social workers were only about 3 per cent better off than they had been in 1913. In the intervening years, moreover, requirements for entering social work had greatly increased.[1]

Although no general study has been made of salaries in relation to the cost of living since 1925, it is believed that salaries continued to increase from 1925 to 1930. The purchasing power of social workers in the latter year was perhaps somewhat greater than it had been in 1925. Subsequent to 1930 many agencies were obliged to reduce salaries, and a second or third reduction was necessary in some. The first decreases were frequently about 10 per cent. Some of these were flat cuts; others were graduated in such a way that

[1] Hurlin, Ralph G., "Social Work Salaries," in The Survey, February 15, 1926, pp. 557 *bis*–558 *bis*.

they worked less hardship on persons in the lower salary brackets. Besides cuts, some of the agencies were obliged to forego the granting of vacations with pay and other privileges.

Salary reductions, economic instability in many of the private agencies, and a consequent sense of insecurity produced unrest, some agitation, and a tendency among certain groups to blame the American Association of Social Workers for not having been so vigilant as it should have been in attempting to safeguard the economic status of the social worker. This disquiet did much to foster the growth of the protective organizations that have already been described. One of their major interests was the economic advancement of their members. Joseph H. Levy, who was active in the movement, wrote of them:

> They regard as false the assumption that a concern with wages and working conditions (or with salaries and standards) is necessarily incompatible with a professional interest in the techniques of social work or that it necessarily clashes with the interests of the community. . . . The new orientation views the social worker as an employe . . . who aside from the nature of the work he may be doing has a legitimate interest in the protection of his standard of living and who may and should use in the protection of that standard an approach that has been found effective by other groups of employes such as teachers and government employes.[1]

As the economic depression gradually receded, financial strain lessened in most of the private agencies and a little improvement, in some instances under pressure from employes, was again made in salaries. In 1938 the median sal-

[1] "New Forms of Organization among Social Workers," in Social Work Today, October, 1934, p. 11.

ary at which family welfare agencies were employing newly hired caseworkers, usually persons with two years of graduate training, was $1,620, while the median for newly hired supervisors was $2,400.[1] Although some of these agencies made provision for raising salaries after a probationary period, and most of them made some increases for tenure, the financial inducement they could offer their employes was not great. It must be recalled, moreover, that family welfare agencies represent a long-cultivated and relatively well-stabilized division of social work.

Salaries in public social work appeared to be even less favorable and to differ greatly from state to state. In the winter of 1938–1939, when representatives of the American Association of Schools of Social Work made investigation of public services in a considerable number of states, they reported that salaries of public assistance investigators ranged from $1,200 to $1,860 annually. Supervisory positions were found to vary from $1,500 to $4,200, but few persons were in the higher brackets. County administrators received from $1,500 to $7,500, depending on the size and nature of the administrative job.[2]

Even in as wealthy and progressive a state as New York, salary figures for November, 1939, for all local public welfare departments, exclusive of New York City, were not encouraging. For 2,279 caseworkers the median salary was $1,457; the salary range was from $900 to $2,900. The 229 case supervisors had a median salary of $2,086 and a

[1] Hurlin, Ralph G., "Recent Hiring Practices of Private Family Agencies," in The Family, October, 1939, p. 183.
[2] American Association of Schools of Social Work, Education for the Public Social Services. University of North Carolina Press, Chapel Hill, 1942, p. 143.

range from $1,200 to $4,000. The median for 82 administrators was $2,167; the range, from $900 to $6,000.[1]

Obviously the salaries paid, particularly those for the operating or "line" positions, have made the maintenance of a professional standard of living difficult. Fortunately, the purchasing power of the dollar had increased substantially after 1929. This had been of great assistance to social workers during the 1930's. But during the latter half of the decade, prices were again rising, while educational requirements were being continuously raised. By late 1941, on the other hand, work in war industries was beginning to provide openings that were attractive to the less well paid social workers and to many who might otherwise have entered the field of social work.

In spite of these several factors which might be expected to result in salary increase, little change has yet been apparent in social work salaries. The most recent salary study is that made by Mr. Hurlin of child-care workers employed in 1941 in 177 private and 26 public child welfare agencies and institutions which are members of or affiliated with the Child Welfare League of America. Information collected through questionnaires revealed that there were some 2,000 professional social work positions in these 203 agencies. Table 10 summarizes the salary data for workers, in some of the more common positions, for whom maintenance was not part of the remuneration received.

It will be seen that, among the members of this national association, the median case-work salary in private child-

1 Figures from a mimeographed report, Salary Levels in Local Administrative Agencies in Upstate New York, November, 1939, Bureau of Research and Statistics, New York State Department of Social Welfare, April 26, 1940.

TABLE 10.—SALARIES IN PRIVATE AND PUBLIC CHILD
WELFARE AGENCIES, 1941[a]

Position and type of agency	Number of workers	Annual salary	
		Median	Range
Executives			
Private agencies or institutions	122	$3,500	$1,620 to $10,200
Child welfare divisions of public welfare departments	20	3,250	1,920 to 7,500
Supervisors and consultants			
Private agencies:			
Directors of case work	12	3,800	2,400 to 5,000
Supervisors of case work	171	2,400	1,640 to 4,000
Public agencies:			
Supervisors of case work	67	2,400	1,800 to 4,500
Inspection and licensing workers	22	2,310	1,680 to 2,940
Case-work consultants	37	2,100	1,620 to 2,700
Caseworkers			
Private agencies	1,100	1,700	840 to 3,000
Public agencies	317	1,620	1,020 to 2,700

[a] Salaries summarized in this table are those of workers who did not receive maintenance as part of salary. Data from a Russell Sage Foundation study, not yet published.

care agencies was $1,700 while the median for the public agencies was $1,620, but this difference may not be significant. The range of salaries in both groups was wide, which may be explained by special circumstances relating to particular positions. For case-work supervisors the median salary in private and public agencies was $2,400. Here the minimum and maximum salaries were higher in the public than in the private agencies, probably because of difference in size of staffs. The median salary for directors of case work in the larger private agencies was $3,800 and the maximum $5,000. No entirely comparable position was recognized for the public agencies. Public case-work consultants are representatives of state child welfare agencies who provide supervision and advisory service for local child welfare agencies. Their salaries tended to be intermediate between those of caseworkers and supervisors directing a case-work staff.

Among 122 executives of the private child-care agencies, men held more of the larger and better paid positions. The median salary for 39 men executives was $5,300; for 83 women it was only $3,300. The salary of one woman executive, however, was $8,000. Of the 20 public agency executives included in the table, only two were men. The median salary for the group was $3,250, or about the same as that for women executives in the private field. It must be borne in mind, however, that most of these 20 executives were, in reality, heads of child welfare divisions within departments of public welfare. Hence their position was, in some respects, more nearly comparable to that of the 12 directors of case work in large private agencies than to the positions occupied by heads of independent private agencies and institutions.

Salary figures invariably raise many questions that are exceedingly difficult to answer. One is of paramount importance to the prospective social worker. Will the salary that he is likely to receive be sufficient to compensate for the time and expense involved in four years of academic preparation and two years of professional training? When Sydnor Walker wrote her book on social work in 1928, she considered salaries so low that adequate preparation was impractical.[1] The same situation exists today over large parts of the United States, if not in general. It applies particularly to the

[1] Social Work and the Training of Social Workers. University of North Carolina Press, Chapel Hill, 1928, pp. 125–127.

South, and to many of the public social services elsewhere. The American Association of Schools of Social Work concluded from its examination of the public services that salary levels were far from commensurate with the financial investment in four years of college followed by two years of professional study.[1]

In spite of prevailing salary scales, the better established agencies have not only placed increasing emphasis upon professional training but have met with considerable success in obtaining workers with such training. Of 398 social workers newly employed in 1938 by private family welfare agencies, 58 per cent had completed graduate training and an additional 31 per cent had had some advanced preparation.[2] In the 203 child-care agencies in 1941, Mr. Hurlin found that 34 per cent of the professional staff had finished graduate training, while 35 per cent offered incomplete advanced preparation. In contrast to these impressive figures, the fact should be recalled that several schools recently created to train social workers particularly for the newer public services have been unsuccessful in recruiting any considerable number of students. Probably because local salaries are so small, college graduates decide that they do not wish to enter the profession.

It must be concluded that salaries have not been large enough to attract many of the more competent and better educated persons, particularly men. On the other hand, it is assumed that salaries generally begin at a higher point for those who have had training in a school of social work than

[1] Education for the Public Social Services, p. 144.
[2] Hurlin, Ralph G., "Recent Hiring Practices of Private Family Agencies," in The Family, October, 1939, p. 183.

for those who have not. Persons with professional preparation, moreover, usually advance more rapidly to supervisory
and executive positions, and hence benefit sooner from better salaries than do those with less educational background.

In his recent study of social workers in children's agencies, Mr. Hurlin correlated professional training and years
of experience with salary. The data of Table 11 illustrate the
results found for professional personnel in 177 private
agencies. This abbreviated table, which concerns only workers with particular lengths of experience, must be interpreted with caution, because the total number of persons included in the study was not large, and because factors that
were not known or could not be evaluated may influence the
figures. The table provides some substantiation, however, of
the general assumption that salaries are higher for those
with professional training than for those with none, not
only at the beginning but throughout the social worker's
career. The table indicates that by the time the social work
graduate has had fifteen years' experience, he has made appreciable relative gains over the untrained person. It is
probable, moreover, that he has not yet reached the peak of
his earning capacity, while the untrained worker has already passed his peak.

Although data are inadequate to provide wholly satisfactory answers to such questions as those of the relation of
social work salaries to the cost of living and to the cost of
professional preparation, progress has been made in obtaining information about salary variations in cities and agencies
of different sizes. As a rule, the agencies of large cities have
larger staffs and pay better salaries than do the agencies of
smaller cities. This is illustrated by Mr. Hurlin's statistics

TABLE II.—RELATION OF PROFESSIONAL TRAINING AND
EXPERIENCE TO SALARY IN PRIVATE CHILD
WELFARE AGENCIES, 1941[a]

Length of experience and school of social work training	Number of workers	Median salary
Less than one year of experience		
Two-year course completed[b]	34	$1,620
Two years; thesis lacking	5	1,500
No school of social work	30	1,080
Three years of experience		
Two-year course completed[b]	48	1,740
Two years; thesis lacking	7	1,620
No school of social work	12	1,280
Five years of experience		
Two-year course completed[b]	60	1,920
Two years; thesis lacking	13	1,800
No school of social work	3	1,500
Ten years of experience		
Two-year course completed[b]	28	2,050
Two years; thesis lacking	5	1,920
No school of social work	5	1,740
Fifteen years of experience		
Two-year course completed[b]	16	2,750
Two years; thesis lacking	7	2,400
No school of social work	10	1,700

[a] From a Russell Sage Foundation study, not yet published.
[b] Category includes some workers with Masters' degrees granted for less than two-year graduate course.

for salaries of all professional workers in 243 private family case-work agencies in 1936.[1] The median salary for executives in cities of under 25,000 population was $2,050, but the median in cities of 500,000 or over was $4,900. The median for supervisors was $2,040 in cities of 75,000 to 100,000 population, but was $3,100 in cities of 500,000 and

[1] Hurlin, Ralph G., "Salaries in Private Family Case Work Organizations in March, 1936," in The Family, December, 1936, p. 254.

over. For caseworkers, the median salary was $1,500 for cities under 25,000 and $1,635 for cities above 500,000.

It would appear that the size of city has much less influence upon salaries of caseworkers than upon those of executives and supervisors. Because the responsibility which caseworkers are expected to assume differs little either among cities, or among agencies of varying sizes, their salaries tend to become more nearly standardized. Among executives and supervisors, however, the degree of responsibility increases with the size of the agency. In this field of social work at least, size of agency appears to influence salaries more than size of city. Median salaries of caseworkers showed progressive increase with size of staff from $1,200 for agencies with only two or three workers, to $1,650 for those with 50 or more workers, while the medians for executives correspondingly increased from $1,800 for the smallest agencies to $5,400 for the larger ones.

Median figures do not, of course, give the complete picture concerning salaries for any of these positions. This is particularly true for the more responsible positions. Thus, in agencies with staffs of 50 or more workers, the range of executives' salaries was from $3,000 to well over $10,000, for assistant executives in charge of case work from $3,300 to $6,000, for case-work supervisors from $1,980 to $5,000, and for district secretaries from $1,500 to $4,300.

It has long been an accepted fact that men in social work are paid much more than are women.[1] The question inevitably arises in regard to the reasons for this difference.

[1] See Deardorff, Neva, "Objectives of the Professional Organization," in Proceedings of the National Conference of Social Work, 1925, p. 642; and Boston Chapter of American Association of Social Workers, A Census of Social Work Positions in Massachusetts, 1932, pp. 19–20.

Studies have shown that men enter social work with some-what less academic education and much less professional training than do women. In recent years, enrollment of men in schools of social work has increased appreciably. In 1940, the last year before the war began to wreck men's careers, nearly one-fourth of those who attended the Association schools, and about a fourth of those who received degrees or certificates upon completion of training, were men.

The chief reason for the great difference which exists in the salary scale for the two sexes is not the inferior preparation of women, but the urgent demand for men for particular positions. They are necessary in those types of social work that are staffed exclusively or predominantly by men. They are wanted as executives and administrators because of their greater influence in the community, particularly in connection with money-raising, promotion of social work plans, and organization of new agencies or strengthening of existing ones. As long ago as 1893, Anna L. Dawes declared that it was desirable to have men as directors of charity organizations. She said, "I do not discuss the reason for this, nor its justice; I simply state it as a fact and I think it cannot be disputed."[1] With the broader role which women are coming to play in all aspects of community and national life, their relative disadvantage in administration and public relations will probably tend gradually to disappear. If that occurs, selection of personnel will need to be based only on competence to "do the job."

As yet, however, emphatic demand for men for highly

[1] "The Need of Training Schools for a New Profession," in Seventh Session of the International Congress of Charities, Correction and Philanthropy, Chicago, June, 1893, p. 15.

responsible positions still exists. Because of it, both private and public agencies have tried to induce them to enter the field by offering executive positions and salaries far in excess of what would be offered women of the same age, education, and experience. Nevertheless, in spite of all efforts, the agencies have not succeeded in recruiting as many or as well-prepared men as they had hoped. All too often inferior men candidates have been given preference over superior women —a situation that has caused bitterness among the latter, but has not resulted in concerted efforts by women to remedy it. Social work is faced with the very important problem of discovering how it can succeed in attracting more men of ability, and how it can persuade them to make adequate preparation for their work.

CURRENT TRENDS IN SOCIAL WORK

As we look back over the four decades of the twentieth century which social work has already traveled, it is apparent that marked progress has been made. No social worker would deny, however, that progress has been at times almost imperceptible and that it has always been laboriously achieved. The great dean of social work, Mary E. Richmond, once said, "A new profession does not come up, like Jonah's gourd, in a night; it is a thing of painfully slow growth." But the slow accretion of the years has begun to make an impressive legacy. The title of a recently published book, From Relief to Social Security, recapitulates the struggle that has been waged and, in large part, won in a particular area of social work.[1]

[1] Abbott, Grace, From Relief to Social Security: the Development of the New Public Welfare Services and Their Administration. Edited by Edith Abbott. University of Chicago Press, Chicago, 1941.

At the turn of the century, assistance to families and to individual persons—known as "poor relief"—was still the responsibility of local governmental units. Obligation for the care of the mentally ill and for defective and delinquent persons had been accepted by the states, but any preventive work undertaken was only of parochial concern. A partnership of federal, state, and county or municipal governments in anything resembling a national welfare program was then unknown. The beginnings of a federal system of employment offices were made in 1907; the first state workman's compensation act was passed in 1910; the first state mother's assistance act in 1911; and the first state old-age pension act in 1914.

By 1939, through the instrumentality of the Social Security Act, the states and the federal government were linked in the administration of public assistance to the aged, the blind, and dependent children; in the provision for special services to children; in the expansion of public health programs; and in the development of unemployment compensation and employment offices. The federal government had assumed responsibility for a national system of old-age insurance. Low-cost housing was being promoted through federal, state, and local co-operation. Nationwide federal work projects to assist unemployed adults capable of working and a federal program of aid to unemployed youth were in operation. Assistance to the unemployable and to other special groups remained the responsibility of local government.[1]

Imperfect and inadequate as are still the social security

[1] American Association of Schools of Social Work, Education for the Public Social Services, pp. 4–6.

services, the expansion of public welfare within our era is an achievement of large proportions. Although countless persons who were not social workers aided in securing the needed legislation, the profession contributed extensively both to the formulation of principles set forth in the Act and to the creation of an informed public opinion. For the determination of administrative policy and rulings, and for the actual execution of the Act, it has assumed still greater responsibility.

But social workers have been even more concerned with the development of the technical content and practice of their profession than with expansion of the social services. They began the present century with almost no body of knowledge or of tradition from which to obtain guidance. Hence social work, of necessity, underwent a period of acute experimentation. From it came varying philosophies and techniques, not all of which were in harmony with one another. Emphasis shifted, methods changed. Social work once meant, for the vast majority of its participants, the administration of relief and concern about the economic causes of poverty and distress. Then case work began to evolve as the social worker's knowledge of human behavior increased, and as psychology, psychiatry, and sociology achieved greater authoritativeness. So completely has the philosophy of case work come to permeate all social work that probably no one within the profession would disagree with Marion Hathway when she says, "The concern of social work is the individual, in the understanding of his needs and in his adjustment to his environment."[1]

[1] "Social Action or Inaction: the Challenge," in Training for Social Work in the Department of Social Science, University of Toronto, 1914–1940, p. 33.

The caseworker responsible for treatment of the unadjusted person has, until recently, helped the client by assembling and analyzing all information available about his present situation; by planning a method of handling this situation through securing the co-operation of family, friends, and employers; and by utilizing the social resources of the community, such as hospitals, clinics, schools, and law courts. Now, however, caseworkers are attempting to encourage the client to assume more responsibility for analysis of his own situation and for planning treatment. This process is, of necessity, complex and difficult. It frequently involves lengthy re-education of the client, which can be achieved only through creation of a relationship between him and the caseworker that is based on understanding and confidence. From the process, the client gains, in the opinion of caseworkers, insight which in itself is of real therapeutic value, and greater ability to meet the exigencies of life.

So valuable a technique has case work proved to be that individualized treatment has been extended, as seen in earlier pages, to a wide variety of philanthropic and publicly financed agencies.[1] Of late there has been growing awareness that a service comparable to that which has proved highly successful in aiding persons in straitened economic circumstances could well be extended on a fee basis to those more fortunately situated. Wartime conditions, which are placing increased pressure on the stability of the family and greater tension on business and industry, have led the Jewish Social Service Association of New York City to conclude that "the time is ripe for case work to be brought

[1] For enumeration of types of agencies, see p. 16.

out of the laboratory of free service, out from its free clinics, built up by philanthropic endeavor, to serve the community at large, those who can pay as well as those who cannot meet the cost of the service."[1] Hence, in the winter of 1942, the Association announced the opening of a Consultation Center, to be operated on a fee basis, without profit, for persons of moderate means.

In an understanding of the individual person, in efforts to aid clients in the solution of problems encountered, and in emphasizing the desirability of individualization of all social services to the greatest possible extent, social work has made marked forward strides. But one serious problem is inevitably encountered, even by caseworkers whose primary interest does not go beyond the perfection of their case-work technique. It is that of a physical and social environment, often distinctly unfavorable to the development of the individual person. So unwholesome is the environment in which vast numbers of persons live that the case-work method—time-consuming and expensive—is, of necessity, limited to a mere fraction of those in need of treatment. When thoughtful observers witness so much energy being expended upon the individual in an effort to make a normal life at all possible for him under bad environmental conditions, some conclude that more emphasis should be placed upon social reform and less upon the welfare of particular persons.

This brings us to that all-important question of the responsibility of the profession of social work for attempting social change. It is a question which was answered in the

[1] "Jewish Social Service Opens a Non-Profit Fee Service," in Better Times, February 13, 1942, pp. 1–2.

nineteenth century by a few courageous souls who embarked on the programs of social reform of that era. With the new conditions of every generation, however, it requires fresh consideration.

In Education for the Public Social Services, the American Association of Schools of Social Work has set down a statement that may be said to represent the current philosophy of social work:

> Social work accepts as its main objective the adjustment of the individual in society. It views this adjustment as dynamic and changing as individual development takes place and as the social setting is modified. It views the lack of adjustment as originating in the physical, mental, and emotional make-up of the individual and in the environment which conditions his behavior. Thus the profession of social work functions in both areas, utilizing certain skills for service to the individual and others for the control of the environment.[1]

In these words the Association asserts recognition of environmental conditions and of certain skills which can be used for control of the environment. In both instances, however, it puts recognition of and attack upon environmental conditions in second place. This does not necessarily result from a belief that external factors are less important than psychological ones in causing maladjustment. But it at least stresses the fact that major reliance is being placed upon treatment of individual rather than social difficulties.

Not long ago, Marshall E. Dimock pointed to the danger that social workers run, because they are so largely concerned with case work, of losing perspective and intimate touch with the larger economic, political, and social problems of which maladjustment of the individual is only a

[1] P. 45.

small part and, in all probability, the direct effect.[1] That, so it seems to some, both within and without the profession, who are deeply interested in the social welfare, is the pitfall that social workers as a whole have only narrowly escaped. Techniques of practice have absorbed the attention both of professional schools and of workers; efforts to improve basic living conditions have been sporadic and have received the active support of only a small part of the profession. And yet the ideology of social work, so Professor Hathway maintains, embraces social action. "Either we accept professional responsibility in relation to the environment and follow the road to the control of forces which threaten to destroy human personality or we admit that the problems are insoluble and become, in the oft-quoted words of Roger Baldwin, 'merely stretcher bearers of industry.' "[2]

Even among those social workers who grant that they should bear whatever responsibility is possible for the improvement of environmental conditions, much discussion has arisen concerning their "area of competence." Such discussion is not always comprehensible to the layman. To refuse to admit an "area of competence," as have some social workers, is to deny the professional base on which social work supposedly rests. To define its inner boundaries, at least, should not be too difficult. Do social workers believe that any other profession is better able to speak authoritatively of need for, and methods of, achieving maintenance of normal family life, protection of children, prevention of

[1] "The Inner Substance of a Progressive," in Social Service Review, December, 1939, p. 577.
[2] "Social Action or Inaction: the Challenge," in Training for Social Work in the Department of Social Science, University of Toronto, 1914–1940, p. 35.

delinquency, extension of public social services including public health and medical care, creation of social group activities, or improvement of housing conditions? To the extent that the solution of these problems is within the competence of any profession, it is certainly within that of social work. These are problems which represent the primary field of responsibility of social workers in social action.

There are other problems which may be considered a secondary field of responsibility: civil liberties, labor legislation, extension of greater economic and social advantages to minority groups, planning for the wiser use of the natural resources and of the labor supply of the United States, and so on. In such questions many individual social workers and some groups are not only deeply interested, but have specific contributions to make. Solution of problems such as these will probably be most effectively achieved by co-operation of social workers with appropriate organizations already established.

Within the area of primary responsibility, however, the question of how specialized knowledge can be translated into productive action is not so easily answered. Fortunately the results of long trial and error and a growing body of knowledge developed by those interested in public opinion are beginning to furnish guide-posts. It is known that many organizations have had a negligible influence because the public suspected them of being inaccurate in the presentation of facts or unsound in the interpretation of those facts. Others, with almost flawless research methods, have had no more influence, because they have failed to make their facts available through channels that would shape public opinion. Some bodies have dissipated their energies and weakened their appeal to society through acting upon large numbers of ill-conceived resolutions, some of which were too insignificant to warrant such formality, while others were too broad in implication to be fully understood even by the constituency of the group.

If social workers are to avoid such errors, the strategy of planning and execution is highly important. The program of social action must be sharply defined and small enough in scope to be manageable. Reference has already been made to the success with which the Delegate Conference of the American Association of Social Workers met in 1936 in Washington, D.C., when it took a vigorous and convincing stand on the subject of relief.[1] That Conference then carried the membership of the Association far in the direction of unified effort toward a national welfare program. But when the Division of Government and Social Work now makes annual recommendations of general principles of national social welfare, there is, it is reported, routine adoption of the recommendations, following discussion devoid of animation or differences of opinion.[2] In the first instance, the Conference had before it a specific proposal for which it could struggle effectively. In the present instance, it is faced with a set of resolutions which, although excellent in themselves, do not lend themselves to concrete and dynamic action.

Social workers should rightfully be, and to some extent are, profoundly interested in the legislative and administrative process as it relates to the improvement and extension

[1] See pp. 127–128.
[2] Hathway, Marion, "Social Action or Inaction: the Challenge," in Training for Social Work in the Department of Social Science, University of Toronto, 1914–1940, pp. 41–42.

of social welfare services. More facilities and personnel are necessary for the preparation of model bills and illustrative administrative rulings, as well as for evaluation of proposed legislation and executive policy. Further channels for communication with the legislative and executive branches of the federal and state governments are also urgently needed.

An even more important undertaking, perhaps, in the field of social action than concern with legislation is creation of a broad and informed public opinion about questions of social welfare. Since it is essential in a democracy, as Dorothy C. Kahn has said, that public opinion determine public policy, "there is greater need than ever for social work to affirm its special knowledge as a determinant in the formation of public policy."[1] Contemporary society is so complicated that it is impossible even for persons of education and good-will to have adequate information about social issues. Pressure groups often contribute only to confusion, since they tend to be more interested in achieving their own ends than in scientific verity. Hence, the building of substantial public opinion is dependent upon the availability and usefulness of facts, correctly, simply, and objectively stated. Considerable progress has been made by private agencies in social work interpretation, and by federal and some state agencies in the collection and dissemination of data relating to social conditions. As yet, however, efforts for the systematic gathering of social facts are few, and techniques for making these facts meaningful to the layman are even less developed. Only to the extent that social work marshals resources for substantial research and effective

[1] "Social Action from the Viewpoint of Professional Organizations," in Proceedings of the National Conference of Social Work, 1940, p. 501.

interpretation will it discharge the responsibility that society entrusts to a profession for the improvement of conditions within the area in which the profession works.

Before bringing this book to a close, something must be said of the situation in which social work finds itself in one of the most critical periods of our history. Even now, nine months after declaration of war by the United States and three years after the beginning of hostilities in Europe, the role of American social work in this world cataclysm is not clear.

One of the great assets which the profession brought to the war is a vastly enlarged structure and a much increased personnel for providing social welfare services. Thanks to the Social Security Act and to other progressive legislation, as well as to a large number of administrative agencies, social work finds itself with most of the requisite organization, not only for continuing public welfare services to the various designated groups, but for extending it to meet the grave vicissitudes which are inevitably arising as the demands of the armed forces and of industry make increased inroads on family and community life. As a consequence, the creation of new social work agencies, with all the attending turmoil, has rarely been necessary. Even the new USO is composed of six national agencies which had had long years of growth and relative stability.

Instead of frantic effort expended on erecting much additional framework, emphasis has been placed upon utilization of available resources. As early as October, 1941, Helen R. Jeter, then executive secretary of the Family Security Committee of the Office of Defense Health and Welfare

Services, remarked, "There are now three slogans for the operation of Federal social services in Washington—'the use of existing agencies,' 'post-emergency planning,' and 'community organization.' "[1] No better example could have been set for the utilization of existing agencies than that of the Family Security Committee itself, composed, as it is, of representatives of all the federal agencies which exercise any functions within the family welfare field and of those national private agencies most intimately concerned with family life.

The War Time Coordinating Committee, created by the Welfare Council of New York City in the spring of 1942, reflects the same tendency to work through established organizations. Its function was described in an early press release as co-ordination by mutual agreement of programs of social and health agencies, in order to strengthen the total preparedness of the city for war. It asserted vigorously that it would discourage the formation of new agencies, unless for clearly needed services which no agency was rendering or could be enabled to render. If an emergency organization were formed, however, the Committee would help it to benefit from the experience of older agencies.[2]

Utilization of existing facilities is in general highly desirable, since duplication of effort is expensive in time and money. Certain questions need, however, to find a more conclusive answer than has yet been afforded them. Is there danger of over-coordination? The tendency to keep planning

[1] Social Work at This Stage of the National Emergency. Mimeographed report of meeting of New York Chapter of American Association of Social Workers, October 27, 1941, p. 3.
[2] Daniels, Frederick I., "To Meet Emergency Needs," in Better Times, March 6, 1942, p. 2.

and control within a relatively small group has often resulted—in business, industry, and the professions alike—in
stifling new ideas, inventions, and creative ways of solving
problems. Is there assurance that co-ordination will result
in strong central leadership which will intelligently determine and promulgate policies and solicit active support?
Unfortunately, persons already overwhelmed with administrative tasks often lack the time and the quietness of mind
necessary for large-scale planning, while latent talents for
leadership are left unexplored.

Are we confident that existing organizations have sufficient flexibility of structure, funds, and personnel to assume
vastly increased responsibilities should they be faced with
urgent and numerous calls for aid? William Hodson's account, reported earlier, of plans for emergency social services in New York City indicates his belief that the Department of Public Welfare, assisted by private agencies, could
answer this question affirmatively.[1]

There has been evidence of a somewhat surprising degree
of flexibility in a few instances where it might not have been
expected. For example, a large number of state or local departments of public welfare early agreed to make investigations of dependency for selective service boards. The Selective Service Act set down no national policy regarding such
investigations. Some departments, furthermore, had always
maintained that their function extended only to administration of public assistance. Yet they willingly entered into co-
operative arrangements because they believed they had a
public service to fulfill in connection with national defense.
As shown by the response to calls for additional service, the

[1] See pp. 162–163.

flexibility of social agencies has probably been generally adequate and sometimes exceptional. On the other hand, the lack of exercise of leadership in initiating plans and services in a period of serious emergency—a deficiency discussed later—has been disappointingly great.

Concerning requisite funds for financing social services, the current picture is confused. Economy-minded groups within the Congress and state legislatures, as well as organizations long interested in decreased taxation, have insisted with some success that those items of the national budget not directly related to the war be drastically reduced. They have maintained that federal agencies like the Civilian Conservation Corps, National Youth Administration, Work Projects Administration, and Farm Security Administration should either be eliminated or their appropriations greatly cut. They have argued that men and women are being drawn into the war effort so rapidly that such undertakings are no longer of urgent necessity; that the American public cannot sustain the crushing burden of financing a worldwide war without rigid economies in civilian services.

There is general agreement throughout the nation that all unnecessary expenditures be eliminated, including the vast sums that still contribute to graft and corruption. But there is serious doubt in the minds of most social workers, as well as of many other informed persons, about the wisdom of crippling the social services, that appear to them to be a base both for improving the public welfare and for helping to win the war. Social workers maintain that decisions regarding fiscal expenditures should rest on attempted objective appraisal of the price that must be paid to sustain necessary morale and unity, and to safeguard those portions of our cultural heritage which are the very antithesis of the patterns of reversion to barbarism that we are fighting to destroy. They recall the unequivocal reply that the great justice, Oliver Wendell Holmes, once gave his legal secretary who inquired if he did not dislike to pay his income tax. "No . . . I like to pay taxes. With them I buy civilization."[1] If the internal welfare of the nation can be thus bought and the chances for external security enlarged through maintenance or expansion, as in England, of the public social services, social workers believe that the majority of persons will, not too unwillingly, find ways to bear the burden of taxation.

Financing of private social work as a whole has yet not been impaired, but probably somewhat improved. The public has contributed with such generosity that 391 community chests, that had completed campaigns by the end of February, 1942, were reported to have raised approximately $4,000,000 more than in 1941.[2] Some organizations whose work is of primary importance but not of wide popular appeal, have been able to maintain their programs to their own surprise. In spite of broad general support of private social work thus far, fear still persists that increased taxation, purchase of war bonds, and voluntary contributions for urgently needed war-relief purposes may ultimately reduce the number and size of gifts for maintenance of established charities. As a result, community chests have occupied themselves with formulation of plans for increasing efficiency in methods of money-raising, and for assuming responsibility

---

[1] Law and Politics: Occasional Papers of Felix Frankfurter, 1913–1938. Edited by Archibald MacLeish and E. F. Prichard. Harcourt, Brace and Co., New York, 1939, p. 78.
[2] "Campaign Results," in Community, March, 1942, p. 112.

for the financial needs of larger numbers of individual agencies.

War chests, administered by representatives of community organizations, are appearing throughout the country. In many cities community chests have already been, or are about to be, merged with these larger fund-raising associations. The success of war chests in the first world conflict has led many war-relief organizations and community chests alike to believe that larger sums of money can thus be obtained, and the public spared the annoyance and confusion of multiple solicitations. Co-ordination of appeals, budgeting, and allocation of funds are progressing rapidly. By presidential order a War Relief Control Board has been created with broad powers to regulate organizations, exclusive of the Red Cross and private social agencies, that are engaged in collecting funds to allay suffering in European countries and in China, and to provide social welfare and recreational facilities for our armed forces. Recently Community Chests and Councils, Inc., has appointed a National Budget Committee for War Appeals to advise local war chests about distribution of money raised in war-relief campaigns. Although these undertakings are outside the area of the financing of private social work, they are, nevertheless, of indirect value in providing community chests with freedom from unplanned competition and with opportunity to work constructively within large inclusive units.

Earlier discussion of personnel requirements led to the conclusion that current demand for social workers is not so great as many persons had expected it to be. Whether the present staffs of the majority of social agencies are adequate to afford any great extension of emergency services is another question. Many state departments of public welfare had been at a distinct disadvantage even before our entrance into the war, because of the extremely low salaries they could offer. In some states they were unable to compete effectively with an occupation as poorly paid as secondary teaching. Now, with remunerative industrial jobs available and with men entering the army and navy, they are experiencing increased difficulty in retaining employes and in making replacements.[1]

Interestingly enough, some existent demand is registered by the federal Civil Service Commission for persons to fill exceptionally good positions in public social work. Administrators of and consultants in public welfare are needed, as are community organizers who have had responsible experience in working with public officials and lay groups. There is also demand for persons who have combined knowledge of social case work, public assistance, and law.[2] Such positions are relatively few in number, and they often remain long unfilled, largely because they require a type of training offered by few professional schools. They are far more important than their number would indicate, however, inasmuch as they are concerned with administration and planning—functions as yet inadequately developed in social work. We can only conclude from such facts about social work that it would find itself in very much straitened circumstances if enormous tasks were cast on it suddenly.

[1] Report by Agnes Van Driel of Family Security Committee to American Association of Schools of Social Work, January 30, 1942. Mimeographed bulletin of Association, no. 2, p. 2.
[2] Report by Elizabeth Cosgrove of the U.S. Civil Service Commission to American Association of Schools of Social Work, January 30, 1942. Mimeographed bulletin of Association, no. 2, p. 1.

In maintaining existing services, in responding to additional calls for aid, and in planning for action under enemy attack, social work has done well. To its credit, moreover, is the sincere desire to be of still greater use. Much time and thought have been expended in attempting to envisage what responsibilities the profession should undertake. But for some not altogether explicable reason, its desire has been frustrated. It has failed as yet to produce the leadership thought possible by many interested persons even outside the profession, who would have liked to see a more positive stand taken concerning the financing of public welfare services; further broadening of the Social Security Act; rapid expansion of social, recreational, and health facilities in the raw industrial communities erupted by the war; and individualized treatment of Japanese-American citizens and of aliens from enemy countries. They would also have favored strong social work support of the Office of Defense Health and Welfare Services as a possible forerunner of a federal department of health and welfare. Albert Deutsch, welfare editor of the newspaper PM, voiced the consensus of such persons when he recently declared, before a council of social agencies, that the response of social work has "been feeble and most disappointing. Where it should lead forcefully, it follows hesitantly."[1]

Among those individuals and groups that have attempted to exercise some leadership, medical social workers should be mentioned. They have now been assigned to base hospital units abroad and their numbers in naval and military hospitals in this country have been appreciably augmented. Of

[1] "Make Plans Now, Deutsch Pleads," in Better Times, June 5, 1942, p. 1.

importance, as indication of initiative and progressive planning, are their experiments in promoting physical rehabilitation of men rejected by selective service boards. They have consistently maintained that the interpretation of physical disability, the explanation of community resources for treatment, and the relief of anxiety and fear concerning ill health are essentially the function of medical social work. In Hartford, Syracuse, Cleveland, and New York workers have effectively insisted that they be given opportunity to demonstrate the validity of their contention.[1] In the first three cities they have been able to offer service, if only on a volunteer basis, under the auspices of health or defense committees or organizations. New York had no agency at all concerned with the rehabilitation of rejectees, and consequently a group of medical social workers decided upon a volunteer demonstration, for a period of six months, that would seek to interest men with obvious physical defects in obtaining medical care, and that would result in procuring data about types of disability and resources available for treatment. No fewer than 300 volunteer social workers, a full-time secretary, and later a paid follow-up worker participated in this demonstration.

If social workers are assuming little leadership in connection with the exigencies of the world crisis, their efforts in preparation for subsequent expansion of social services to war-torn countries are even less impressive. Some individual social workers are contributing time, money, and experience to organizations established for the study of problems of post-war social reconstruction. But the profession as such

[1] Soule, Theodate H., "Selective Service," in Bulletin of the American Association of Medical Social Workers, April, 1942, pp. 14–17.

has done nothing to create an appropriate organization of its own, or to establish a roster of persons with international experience or with social work training accompanied by a knowledge of foreign languages, who would be called on, if necessary, to initiate programs of public welfare and health services abroad. Yet, it cannot safely assume that the American Red Cross and the American Friends Service Committee can bear the entire burden, particularly in countries like Poland, Czechoslovakia, and Greece, that are fast being despoiled not only of social welfare workers but of their entire intellectual class.

Several universities are already offering courses designed to provide understanding of social problems that have sprung from the war. Others, like Columbia University, are planning more specific training for persons who wish to prepare themselves for reconstruction tasks. Schools of social work have issued no announcement of professional training directed toward international public welfare, in spite of the fact that scores of European welfare workers, thoroughly conversant with the social and economic structure of their own countries, are available for teaching purposes. Some persons even, who have sought to enroll in the regular curriculum of schools of social work as preparation for such foreign service, have been rejected, because they were unable to meet all technical admission requirements. If any institutions of higher learning and any professional bodies have responsibility for preparations to restore some semblance of well-being and security to a suffering humanity, they are, first and foremost, those whose basic concern is "the adjustment of the individual in society."

APPENDIX

EVOLVING CURRICULA OF SOCIAL WORK, NOT MEMBERS OF AMERICAN ASSOCIATION OF SCHOOLS OF SOCIAL WORK

(For definition of Groups I, II, III, IV, and reason for assignment of individual schools to these groups, see pp. 31–39.)

GROUP I

BELOW are listed 22 colleges and universities that announced in their bulletins, generally for the academic year 1941–1942, a curriculum in social work. In 10 institutions, training was exclusively or predominantly on a graduate basis; in eight both undergraduate and graduate instruction were offered; in four it was almost exclusively undergraduate. Six of these 22 institutions specialized in training personnel for Y.M.C.A. and other group work and for church social work.

A brief statement concerning each of these curricula has been prepared from the bulletins, supplemented, whenever possible, by letters received from the administrative officers whose names appear after those of the institutions. Omission of a name indicates that requested information was not provided.

ADELPHI COLLEGE, GRADUATE SCHOOL OF SOCIAL WORK, GARDEN CITY, N.Y.

In 1941–1942 a five-year program of preprofessional and professional training was instituted. The one-year graduate curriculum was designed to lead to a professional certificate in social work, and to the master's degree upon completion of additional graduate courses approved by the College.

The graduate course of study conforms, in general outline, to that of the minimum curriculum recommended by the American Association of Schools of Social Work.

No information obtainable by correspondence about the number of students enrolled or prospective plans.

ALABAMA, UNIVERSITY OF, DEPARTMENT OF SOCIOLOGY, TUSCALOOSA. E. W. GREGORY, JR., PROFESSOR OF SOCIOLOGY

Professional courses in introduction to social case work, field practice in social case work, and public welfare administration offered only during summer session to a maximum of 20 qualified college graduates, who have completed a minimum of 30 semester hours of undergraduate work in the social and biological sciences, of which at least 12 must have been in sociology.

This curriculum is approved by the Alabama State Department of Public Welfare, and students completing the courses are qualified to take the merit board examinations for the position of caseworker.

The University hopes to expand the curriculum to at least one year of training in the regular session as soon as it can be done on a thoroughly sound basis.

ARKANSAS, UNIVERSITY OF, DEPARTMENT OF SOCIAL WELFARE, FAYETTEVILLE. MRS. MATTIE C. MAXTED, ASSISTANT PROFESSOR OF SOCIAL WELFARE

Department organized in 1940–1941. Seventy students enrolled in winter of 1942, of whom 20 were majors in the department. Only two were graduate students. One full-time teacher. Course in community organization taught by Department of Sociology. Three persons in local welfare agencies help to supervise a small number of students in limited type of field work.

The University believes it possible to develop a substantial school on the undergraduate level. Since salaries are very low and the majority of social workers have only a high school education, an attempt to offer graduate training exclusively is considered inappropriate at the present time.

EVOLVING CURRICULA

FLORIDA STATE COLLEGE FOR WOMEN, DEPARTMENT OF SO-
CIOLOGY AND SOCIAL WORK, TALLAHASSEE. COYLE E. MOORE,
ASSOCIATE PROFESSOR OF SOCIOLOGY AND DIRECTOR OF SO-
CIAL WORK

Some training has been offered on undergraduate level to from
10 to 25 students annually for ten years. This training has
been considered inadequate by the College, but salaries have
been low and local demands have been for workers with a
"little" training.

In 1939 a one-year graduate curriculum was established, designed to meet the requirements for a Type I school of the
American Association of Schools of Social Work. Ten students, some on a part-time basis, enrolled in 1941–1942. Director believes that since the demand for social workers is increasing in Florida, enrollments would increase rapidly were
the school accepted for membership in the national association.

ILLINOIS, UNIVERSITY OF, CURRICULUM IN SOCIAL ADMINIS-
TRATION, URBANA. PROFESSOR B. F. TIMMONS, CHAIRMAN OF
SOCIAL ADMINISTRATION COMMITTEE

Five-year curriculum leading to degree of Bachelor of Social
Administration introduced in 1939–1940. A carefully designed preprofessional sequence of courses offered, extending over four years. Students who successfully completed this
sequence might enroll for the fifth year, which consisted of
professional courses planned to conform to the requirements
for Type I school of the Association of Schools.

Training specifically adapted to meet Illinois requirements for
public welfare workers. Partly because of the small salaries
paid by the state, enrollments were disappointingly small.
Nineteen matriculated in the professional curriculum in second semester of 1941–1942, only two of whom were full-
time students. Extension courses also offered in neighboring
cities and in Springfield. Twenty persons were enrolled in one
course in winter of 1942; 14, in another. Plans now being
made either for discontinuance or reorganization of school.

SOCIAL WORK AS A PROFESSION

KENTUCKY, UNIVERSITY OF, DEPARTMENT OF SOCIAL WORK, LEXINGTON. VIVIEN M. PALMER, HEAD OF DEPARTMENT OF SOCIAL WORK

Courses in social work, either on undergraduate or graduate level, offered continuously since 1918. From 1935 to 1939 a limited curriculum, offered by the Department of Sociology, was accredited for junior membership in the American Association of Social Workers. In 1939 Department of Social Work was established, designed to meet requirements for Type I school of the American Association of Schools of Social Work.

During academic year 1940–1941, 25 graduate students were enrolled for credit of whom six were full-time, and 17 were employed social workers. Five certificates awarded. Fifteen students were enrolled in preprofessional curriculum which included 15 semester hours of introduction to social work.

MICHIGAN STATE COLLEGE, GRADUATE CURRICULUM IN SOCIAL WORK, DEPARTMENT OF SOCIOLOGY, EAST LANSING. ERNEST B. HARPER, HEAD OF DEPARTMENT

In 1936 a technical course was instituted for seniors in the undergraduate curriculum, designed primarily as training for emergency relief work. In 1940 a one-year curriculum on the graduate level was introduced, planned to meet the requirements for Type I school of the American Association of Schools of Social Work, but with emphasis on training for county welfare positions. Graduates eligible to take merit examination for Social Worker A or B.

Appreciable drop in enrollment when training was shifted from undergraduate to graduate basis. Five certificates awarded in 1940–1941.

MILLS COLLEGE, GRADUATE CURRICULUM IN SOCIAL WORK, OAKLAND, CALIF. AURELIA HENRY REINHARDT, PRESIDENT

The following is a résumé of the statement appearing in the Mills College Bulletin for 1940–1941. Because of the outbreak of war, expected financial assistance for the development of program was not obtainable. Hence expansion may have to await more favorable conditions.

Graduates of approved colleges, who have completed major sequences in one of the biological or social sciences, or in physical education, may be admitted to the two-year curriculum in social work leading to the degree of Master of Arts. Graduates of Mills College may qualify for admission to the curriculum in social work through the general major in the Social Services or through an undergraduate sequence in one of the above named sequences.

The Graduate Curriculum in Social Work is intended (1) to provide professional education at the graduate level for women desiring to enter the California public welfare services or to work with private social agencies; (2) to provide an opportunity for advanced study, including practical experience, for those who are looking forward to the development of improved social welfare standards in California; and (3) to co-operate in social research with the social agencies and public welfare organizations, especially those in the San Francisco Bay region.

The minimum period of registration and study required to complete the curriculum leading to the degree of Master of Arts shall be three semesters. The specific program of study in social work shall include: theory of social work, one course; psychiatry in social work, one-half course; a graduate seminar in the field of major emphasis, one course; supervised field training in social work, one course; elective, one course. A thesis may be required at the option of the Director of the Graduate Curriculum in Social Work, and may count as one of the one and one-half graduate courses required within the school.

MISSOURI, UNIVERSITY OF, DEPARTMENT OF SOCIOLOGY, COLUMBIA. MORRIS S. WORTMAN, INSTRUCTOR IN SOCIOLOGY

In addition to large number of courses in sociology, the following in social welfare are listed: field of social work, case work I and II, community organization for social work, public welfare administration, social legislation, medical information for social workers. All given on undergraduate level.

Reported that from 40 to 50 students enrolled, in second semester of 1942, in one or more courses. This was a 50 per cent increase over preceding year.

University held membership in American Association of Schools of Social Work until the national body raised requirements to at least one year of graduate work. Both Department of Sociology and University have long wished to establish graduate curriculum, but state appropriations have not been made.

NORTH DAKOTA, UNIVERSITY OF, COURSE IN SOCIAL WORK OF DEPARTMENT OF SOCIOLOGY, GRAND FORKS. PROFESSOR T. W. CAPE, DIRECTOR

Pre-Professional Social Work Curriculum, offered to juniors and seniors, includes courses in social sciences, biology, introduction to social work, and introduction to public welfare. In February, 1942, enrollment was 33.

Professional Course in Social Work open to graduate students with adequate preprofessional training or experience in social work, and to qualified seniors. Following courses offered: social case work, advanced social case work, child welfare case work, field practice in social case work, field practice in child welfare case work, public welfare administration, medical information for social workers, community organization, county welfare organization, social work statistics, social security. Enrollment: graduate students, 17; undergraduate, 15. Employed social workers constituted about 25 per cent of enrollment.

Decreased enrollment in professional courses expected during war, as men are entering military service and women find more remunerative employment.

No certificate or other form of specific recognition has yet been given. Director reports, however, that he expects present curriculum to develop into accredited one-year professional school. No specialized field agencies for more advanced professional courses.

NOTRE DAME, UNIVERSITY OF, DEPARTMENT OF SOCIAL WORK, NOTRE DAME, IND. FRANK T. FLYNN, HEAD

Curriculum had been evolved, with emphasis on training for work with delinquents and in public welfare, that was designed to meet the requirements for Type I school of the American Association of Schools of Social Work. Application had been filed for membership in the Association. In January, 1942, the University, which accepts only men students, decided to discontinue the Department for the duration of the war. In November, 1940, 12 full-time graduate students and 5 part-time had been enrolled. In November, 1941, there were 7 full-time and 3 part-time students.

SOUTH CAROLINA, UNIVERSITY OF, SCHOOL OF SOCIAL WORK, COLUMBIA. GEORGE CROFT WILLIAMS, DIRECTOR OF SCHOOL

Organized in 1934, through assistance of the federal government, to train workers for Federal Emergency Relief Administration. South Carolina subsequently established Department of Public Welfare which needs trained workers, and local agencies are becoming increasingly aware of desirability of professional personnel. Faculty of School has assisted in upbuilding of those private agencies in which students carry on their field work.

Although School is designed to be on graduate level, it is not yet possible to attract sufficient students for advanced training. Hence, seniors, who have completed other college requirements including requisite work in the social sciences, are admitted, as are eligible employed social workers.

Courses offered are as follows: introductory family case work, advanced case work, child welfare, children's case work, medical information, psychiatric information, social research, direction of leisure-time activities, social problems of labor, public welfare administration, case work in institutions and schools. Three hundred hours of field work required.

Enrollment, as of February, 1942, was 23; undergraduates, 14; graduates, 7; special students, 2. In 1941, 6 students received A.B. degree; 3, Master of Social Service.

TEMPLE UNIVERSITY, DEPARTMENT OF SOCIAL GROUP WORK OF TEACHERS COLLEGE, PHILADELPHIA

Department was instituted to provide professional training for employment in social group-work agencies, social educational programs of church centers, government programs of recreation and adult education, extension divisions of public schools, adult education programs under auspices of private agencies, community councils, and councils of social agencies.

Two curricula offered. First, two-year program with emphasis on supervised field work as well as theory, designed for qualified graduate students, leading to degree of Master of Education and to certificate in group work. Second, five-year curriculum open to secondary school graduates of high standing. B.S. in Education awarded at end of four years; Master of Education and certificate at end of fifth year, provided student has satisfactorily completed courses outlined. Single courses and seminars provided for practicing group workers and teachers.

According to Bulletin for March, 1941, following courses were offered both to graduate and undergraduate students: principles of social group work, observation and leadership in group-work agencies [field work], group aspects of parent education, social aspects of adult education, methods and materials of adult education, summer field work in social group-work agencies, adult civic education, the individual and his adjustment, counseling and guidance, social treatment of problems of youth, skills and program resources for group worker, social aspects of leisure, foreign communities and immigration.

The following courses were designed for graduate students only: research seminar, the institutional survey, supervision in social group work, advanced field work in social group-work agencies, administration of social agencies, advanced seminar in social group work, social case work for the group worker, field work in case work, community organization, the survey and community analysis.

No report available concerning number of students.

UTAH STATE AGRICULTURAL COLLEGE, GRADUATE DIVISION OF SOCIAL WORK, LOGAN. PROFESSOR JOSEPH A. GEDDES, DIRECTOR

One-year graduate school designed expressly to train men and women for rural social work, since the school of social work of the University of Utah prepares primarily for urban positions. Curriculum drafted to conform with standards set by American Association of Schools of Social Work. Extensive undergraduate training in social sciences required for admission. Certificate in social work awarded upon completion of curriculum. Eleven regular graduate students enrolled in March, 1942. Two or three others permitted to take special courses.

A joint committee, representing the University of Utah and the State College, now studying, at request of governor, question of duplication of work in the two schools. Hence, future of this school is uncertain.

WISCONSIN, UNIVERSITY OF, DEPARTMENT OF SOCIOLOGY AND ANTHROPOLOGY, MADISON. HELEN I. CLARKE, ASSISTANT PROFESSOR OF SOCIAL WORK

Training has been given largely on undergraduate level, because of previous inability of Department to obtain funds for the creation of a graduate school of social work. Since Wisconsin has no reservoir of trained social workers, both Department and State Conference of Social Work are requesting expanded facilities for professional education to meet the regular and emergency needs of state.

Large numbers of students take undergraduate courses in theory. In February, 1942, 10 seniors and graduate students were doing field work in City Relief Department, and 20 in group-work agencies. Courses in psychiatry for social workers and public welfare administration, given on graduate level, were open to employed social workers as well as to seniors and graduate students.

XAVIER UNIVERSITY, SCHOOL OF SOCIAL SERVICE, NEW ORLEANS

School founded in 1934 for the training of Negro men and women social workers.

Two-year course, leading to a certificate upon completion of first year and a diploma or M.S. upon completion of second year.

Curriculum planned in accordance with standards set by American Association of Schools of Social Work. Courses for first year include those of the minimum curriculum adopted by the Association. Those listed for second year, in Bulletin of January, 1942, include advanced case work and field work, group work, social research, history of social work, social insurance, legal aspects of social work, community organization, housing problems.

College of Liberal Arts offers courses in School for undergraduates who may take a major or minor in social service. These courses are separate from those on the professional, graduate level.

No report available on number of students enrolled.

COLLEGES OFFERING TRAINING FOR Y.M.C.A. AND OTHER GROUP WORK OR FOR CHURCH SOCIAL WORK

GEORGE WILLIAMS COLLEGE, PROFESSIONAL DIVISION, CHICAGO. DONALD M. TYPER, VICE-PRESIDENT

Founded in 1890 to provide professional training for personnel of Y.M.C.A. Made coeducational in 1933–1934, and scope of work broadened to offer preparation for all types of group-work agencies.

Undergraduate program of *three* years, beyond the Junior College, leads to B.S. in Group Work Education, or in Group

Work Administration. Graduate program of two years leads to M.S. in the two specialties. Graduate diploma is also offered to those not fulfilling certain specified requirements for the M.S. Applicant who holds the professional B.S. degree from the College may normally complete graduate work in one year.

Large number of courses offered on graduate level as well as on undergraduate. Three courses in supervision, guidance, and current political and economic trends affecting social agencies, also being offered in downtown Chicago as extension courses. Twenty-seven social workers enrolled for graduate credit.

In February, 1942, enrollments on campus were as follows: undergraduates in professional division in Group Work Education and Group Work Administration, 51; first-year graduate students, 19; second year, 14. Of the total of 84, 64 were men and 20 were women. In 1941, 25 degrees were conferred: 17 B.S. and 8 M.S. degrees.

SCARRITT COLLEGE FOR CHRISTIAN WORKERS, DEPARTMENT OF SOCIAL WORK, NASHVILLE. LORA LEE PEDERSON, PROFESSOR OF SOCIAL WORK

Scarritt Bible and Training School opened in 1892 in Kansas City for training women as foreign missionaries of the Methodist Episcopal Church, South. Moved in 1924 to Nashville where curriculum was expanded to include training of men and women church workers. College now admits only students who have completed two years of college. Provides senior college work leading to B.A. and graduate work leading to M.A. for those interested in church and community work, foreign missions, religious education and teaching, and social work.

In social work all courses are open both to senior and graduate students, except the preprofessional course, introduction to social work, and a seminar in social work scheduled only for graduate students. The following courses are noted in catalogue:

Case Work: social case work; field work in case work, medical information, legal aspects of social work.

Group Work: principles of group work, group skills, camp craft, field work in group work, supervision in social group work.

Organization and Administration: the settlement, community organization, seminar in social work.

No report available of number of students enrolled in social work.

At present plans are being made for a graduate school of social work to be operated jointly by Scarritt College, Vanderbilt University, and George Peabody College.

SCHAUFFLER COLLEGE OF RELIGIOUS AND SOCIAL WORK, CLEVELAND. EARL VINIE, PRESIDENT

Undergraduate college conferring degree of B.S. in Religious Education or Church Social Work. In January, 1942, 30 students were majoring in church social work. No training for secular social work. Eight part-time faculty members teach courses in church social work, all of whom are employed in Cleveland social agencies. Six to nine hours of field work weekly under supervision of a half-time teacher. Other courses include fields of social work, social case work, child welfare, medical information for social workers, psychiatric information for social workers, group leadership, principles of group work, community organization.

No plans being made to introduce church social work on graduate level. Rather is an effort being made to strengthen the undergraduate curriculum and to re-orient training for the "rebuilding of the social order." As a first step in the process, an experimental course, required of all seniors, has been introduced in community church relations.

SPRINGFIELD COLLEGE, SOCIAL SCIENCE DIVISION, SPRING-FIELD, MASS. LAWRENCE K. HALL, DIRECTOR OF DIVISION

College established in 1885 as training center for executives of Y.M.C.A. Under the Five-Year Plan of Professional Study, now offered, student may receive bachelor's degree at end of fourth year, and master's degree or certificate or both at end of fifth year.

Social Science Division provides general and professional preparation for positions in Y.M.C.A.'s, boys' clubs, settlements, recreation centers, churches, and so on. Beginning with junior year, the work of the Division is offered in three programs of study: group-work education, counseling and guidance, religious education.

Director of Division reported 32 seniors in group work, and five in counseling and guidance in January, 1942. There were five fifth-year students. Number of latter had decreased sharply because of draft. Demand of Y.M.C.A.'s and other social agencies for persons with only baccalaureate degree, moreover, is so great that difficulty is experienced in keeping students for fifth year.

WHITTIER COLLEGE, Y.M.C.A. GRADUATE TRAINING FOR SEC-
RETARYSHIP, WHITTIER, CALIF. HARRY F. HENDERSON, ACT-
ING DEAN OF Y.M.C.A. TRAINING

In 1931 Whittier College, organized by the Society of Friends more than forty years earlier, was designated as an official secretarial training school for Y.M.C.A. Training offered only on undergraduate level until 1941–1942, when a fifth year was added. Y.M.C.A. Credential will now be awarded only upon completion of one year of graduate work. Thus it is hoped that a large percentage of students, in peacetime, will take the additional training. Twenty students enrolled in undergraduate training in autumn, 1941.

Training program not considered that of a school of social work, but Dean believes that group workers should have some knowledge of generic social work. Training taken by some prospective Boy Scout leaders. Required curriculum for graduate year includes: principles of group work, organization and administration of social agency, philosophy of social work, supervised field work, adaptation of physical education to Y.M.C.A., supervision of group work, administration of Y.M.C.A., counseling clinic.

WILLAMETTE UNIVERSITY, DEPARTMENT OF SOCIOLOGY, SA-
LEM, ORE. S. B. LAUGHLIN, PROFESSOR OF SOCIOLOGY AND
ANTHROPOLOGY

Some undergraduate social work training is offered, and the establishment of a graduate school of social work is under consideration. Recently the University has been designated as an official center for preparation of Y.M.C.A. secretaries, and a curriculum for such training has been instituted.

Undergraduate courses, offered by the Department of Sociology and Anthropology in co-operation with the Marion County Public Welfare Commission, include introduction to social work, introduction to social case work, introduction to social psychiatry, applied social psychiatry, the community, domestic relations, and public welfare laws.

The training course for leadership in the Y.M.C.A. is as follows: *Senior year:* sociology seminar, education, public administration, international relations, physical education, social case work, group work, counseling and guidance, development of Y.M.C.A. movement. *Fifth year:* the community, supervised Y.M.C.A. practice, organization and administration of social and religious organizations, administration of Y.M.C.A.'s, social or religious research; field practice in the Salem and Portland Y.M.C.A.'s.

Because of extensive reorganization which Willamette has been undergoing, no information is available concerning number of social work or Y.M.C.A. students enrolled in 1941–1942.

GROUP II

Included in Group II are 14 colleges and universities that announce a sequence of courses in social work, generally offered by departments of sociology or of social science. These courses are predominantly undergraduate, but occasionally some graduate instruction is added.

Statements appearing below were prepared from the most

216

recent bulletins available, generally those for 1941–1942. They were then sent to the respective institutions for approval. In a few instances no reply was received, and consequently some of the statements are without verification.

AKRON, UNIVERSITY OF, AKRON, OHIO

Within Department of Sociology, juniors and seniors may elect sequence of courses in social welfare as field of concentration. Technique of social case work, theory of social work, government and social welfare, sanitation, community organization, child welfare, welfare aspects of social security, and statistics are required courses. One hundred fifty hours of field work are also required in senior year in case-work or group-work agencies.

Several of the courses are planned to meet needs of employed social workers as well as students.

ALABAMA COLLEGE [THE STATE COLLEGE FOR WOMEN], MONTEVALLO

Within the Department of Sociology and entirely on undergraduate level are four courses in social case work, two in employment interviewing, and one each in community organization and public welfare. A special field-work unit is maintained in co-operation with the Shelby County Department of Public Welfare, whereby students work under supervision on cases involving case-work problems. In a course dealing with problems affecting school attendance, students act as attendance officers for part of county.

GEORGIA STATE COLLEGE FOR WOMEN, MILLEDGEVILLE

In Department of Social Sciences are included courses in field of social work, problems of child welfare, community organization, social legislation and theories of social reform, public welfare administration, and introduction to social case work.

Bulletin refers to Program of Public Welfare and Social Service, designed for those who wish to pursue studies in a graduate school of social work or to enter social work immediately in rural and small-town communities. Program not outlined, but obviously refers to courses listed above, plus work in social science.

JOHN CARROLL UNIVERSITY, CLEVELAND

Among the many courses offered by the Department of Sociology on an undergraduate basis are the following: history of social work, principles of social case work, community organization, public welfare, social legislation, social and economic reforms [based on encyclicals of Leo XIII and Pius XI], social statistics, child welfare, psychology of character [for group workers], mental hygiene, social psychiatry.

MARQUETTE UNIVERSITY, MILWAUKEE

Undergraduate social work courses offered by the Department of Sociology include: introduction to social work, social case work, child welfare, community organization, social field work, theory and history of play, function of play, home and school recreation, and community recreation. Field work in the various social agencies of Milwaukee provides student with basis for deciding whether he wishes to continue studies in graduate school.

MONTANA, UNIVERSITY OF, MISSOULA

Among the undergraduate courses in sociology given are the following in social work: principles of social case work, community organization, field work in social administration, child welfare, public welfare administration, administration of public assistance. Advanced field work in social administration is offered graduate students who have already had principles of social case work.

MOUNT SAINT MARY'S COLLEGE, LOS ANGELES

In Department of Sociology following undergraduate courses are given: history of social work, theory and philosophy of play and group work, psychiatric aspects of social work, social surveys and research, medical social service, problems of child welfare, fundamentals of social work, social group work and leadership, introduction to social case work, methods of social case work (including field work).

NEW HAMPSHIRE, UNIVERSITY OF, DURHAM

Social Service Curriculum, extending over the four undergraduate years, has been designed as broad preparation for a two-year professional course in an approved school. Where such professional training is impossible, this curriculum is intended to provide fundamentals and technique for certain types of positions, particularly in rural areas. Those students who desire supervised urban training may take three years at the University and the fourth at an approved school of social work. The University degree will be awarded at end of fourth year.

In the junior year, in addition to courses in the social sciences, there are offered: methods of social research, methods of social case work, and psychopathology or mental hygiene. In senior year, courses are given in sociological research, social service and field work, recreation and leisure, and methods of social progress. It is recommended that students spend the summer preceding senior year working under supervision in an urban social agency.

OHIO UNIVERSITY, ATHENS

Within the Department of Sociology which provides a wide variety of courses, the following in social work are listed for advanced undergraduate and graduate students: child welfare, public assistance, public welfare administration, introduction to case work, advanced case work, visiting teacher, rural survey and planning, social research. Field work is offered under the following bulletin headings: juvenile court services, internship training in juvenile courts, child welfare services, family welfare services, institutional social service.

SAINT MICHAEL'S COLLEGE, WINOOSKI PARK, VT.

A major sequence in sociology and social work is being developed in this undergraduate college, which enrolls men students, and religious sisters during the summer session. In addition to a few courses in sociology and other social sciences, the following social work courses are offered: social case work, philosophy of social work, social [Catholic] ethics, field work, seminar in social work. It was announced that the following would be added in 1942–1943: history of social work, public welfare, social legislation, community organization for social work, financing private social work, medical information for case work, social statistics.

SAM HOUSTON STATE TEACHERS COLLEGE, HUNTSVILLE, TEXAS

Undergraduate curriculum of social work has been established with prescribed courses for the four years. In addition to required work in sociology and the other social sciences, following courses are offered: introduction to social work, social work techniques, sociology of public welfare, field work.

SAN FRANCISCO STATE COLLEGE, SAN FRANCISCO

A major in social service is offered: to provide a background for case and group workers; to furnish undergraduate preparation for advanced study in social work or sociology; to aid those who wish to take civil service examinations or to serve as volunteer workers and as members of boards of social agencies. The major meets the requirements for the credential in child welfare and supervision of attendance.

In addition to specified courses in the social sciences, courses are offered in theory of social case work, social case practice, problems of the family, standards of living, labor problems.

SOUTH DAKOTA, UNIVERSITY OF, VERMILLION

A major in social work offered on undergraduate level. Courses include introduction to social work, introduction to field work, social security, public welfare, advanced field work, group work, social statistics, child welfare, and social agencies.

TEXAS CHRISTIAN UNIVERSITY, FORT WORTH

Division of Social Welfare, within the Department of Sociology, offers the following courses: foundations of social work, introduction to social work, social case study, child welfare, organizing the community, national defense and social welfare, group work, and social psychiatry. All these courses, except child welfare given by the Department of Sociology, are offered in the evening for credit and are taught by employed social workers.

GROUP III

Below are listed 18 institutions of higher learning whose bulletins, in most instances for the academic year 1941–1942, note three or four undergraduate courses in social work.

Albion College, Albion, Mich. [Group work exclusively]
Birmingham-Southern College, Birmingham
College of the Pacific, Stockton, Calif.
Colorado State College, Fort Collins
D'Youville College, Buffalo
Idaho, University of, Moscow
Immaculate Heart College, Los Angeles
Kalamazoo College, Kalamazoo, Mich.
Marygrove College, Detroit
Saint Bonaventure College, Saint Bonaventure, N.Y.
Saint Joseph College [for Women], West Hartford, Conn.
Saint Mary's College, Notre Dame, Holy Cross Post Office, Ind.
Southern Methodist University, Dallas
Syracuse University, Syracuse
Toledo, University of, Toledo, Ohio

Villa Maria College, Erie, Pa.
Virginia Union University [Negro], Richmond
Winthrop College [The South Carolina College for Women],
  Rock Hill

GROUP IV

Departments of sociology of some 94 colleges and universities announced in recent bulletins an undergraduate course designed to survey the field of social work. In several instances a second course was noted, and sometimes a third, the content of which might be predominantly either social work or sociology.

INDEXES

INDEX OF SUBJECTS

INDEX OF AUTHORS

(Some of the names included in this index are of faculty members of schools of social work who are noted, not in the role of authors, but for the contribution they are making to the curricula of their schools.)